RELIGION IN LIFE CURRICULUM
Edited by Edward A. Fitzpatrick, Ph.D.

THIRD GRADE TEACHERS PLAN BOOK
AND MANUAL

HIGHWAY TO HEAVEN SERIES

BOOK OF THE HOLY CHILD (Grade One)

LIFE OF MY SAVIOR (Grade Two)

LIFE OF THE SOUL (Grade Three)

BEFORE CHRIST CAME (Grade Four)

THE VINE AND THE BRANCHES (Grade Five)

THE MISSAL (Grade Six)

HIGHWAY TO GOD (Grades Seven and Eight)

Accompanying this Series is the RELIGION IN LIFE CURRICULUM for grades one to six and PRACTICAL PROBLEMS IN RELIGION for grades seven and eight.

Religion in Life Curriculum

Third Grade Teachers Plan Book and Manual

Designed for use with the
HIGHWAY TO HEAVEN SERIES
of Catechism Textbooks

ST. AUGUSTINE ACADEMY PRESS
HOMER GLEN, ILLINOIS

Nihil obstat:
  H. B. RIES,
    Censor librorum

Imprimatur:
  ✝ SAMUEL ALPHONSUS STRITCH
    Archiepiscopus Milwaukiensis

February 14, 1933

This book was originally published in 1933 by The Bruce Publishing Company.
This edition reprinted in 2018 by St. Augustine Academy Press.
ISBN: 978-1-64051-028-9

INTRODUCTION

There is presented herewith the teacher's plan book and manual for the third grade of the curriculum in religion. In the first two grades the whole life of Christ was presented; the childhood of Christ in the first grade, and the public life of Christ in the second grade. Having built up motives for the love of God and of His Divine Son, Jesus Christ, on the knowledge of Christ in the first two grades, the third grade reviews the facts of the life of Christ and the plan of Redemption. Fuller knowledge is given of the doctrine of the sacraments and more particularly of the four sacraments which especially concern children.

Here we see more definitely the cumulative and progressive character of this curriculum. We see doctrine grow in definiteness and richness, even though it is not the sole, or always the central interest. Here we see children building up a certain and broad base of knowledge for the faith that is in them. Here we see the beginnings of a real Catholic culture, including in an organized life the core of theological doctrine, religious poetry and hymnology, religious practice, life situations guided by religion, religious art, and the liturgy. It is this organization of the Christian Catholic life that is the central motive of this course. It is this objective that must be achieved if a course in religion justifies itself.

Many priests and sisters coöperated in the preparation of this work. Sister Mary Angela King, S.S.N.D., helped much, but special thanks are due to Sister Mary Agnesine, S.S.N.D., for the practical character and final form of the work of this grade.

EDWARD A. FITZPATRICK.

EDITOR'S NOTE TO THE REPRINTED EDITION:

In reassembling this *Religion in Life Curriculum*, we thought it best to include excerpts from the curriculum overview volume, titled *Curriculum in Religion*, which was published in 1931 as the basis for development of the fleshed-out Teachers Plan Book and Manual before you. In that original volume, the entire curriculum for first through eighth grades were laid out in basic outline form, with attention given to the main focus, goals and resources for each grade. You may find that some of the resources listed in these excerpts did not find their way into the current manual. However, we felt it would be helpful to the teacher (or parent) to see a summary of the intended vision for the current year.

In the appendix found at the rear of this volume, we have also provided a comprehensive listing of all the recommended resources found in this manual, to which we have added notations showing the most frequently used and/or most helpful resources, as well as those which can be found online.

Lastly, please note that most of the recommended student readings (that is, those which would have been found in the various school readers listed throughout this book) have been assembled and printed under one cover in the new *Magnificat Readers* which accompany this series. In addition, we have done our best to find and scan the pages of *The Catholic School Journal* and *The Journal of Religious Instruction* recommended herein; find these on our website at www.staapress.com/hth-teacher-resources.

Lisa Bergman

St. Augustine Academy Press
February 2018

CONTENTS

Page

INTRODUCTION v

SUGGESTIONS FOR THE TEACHER xxxi

TIME ALLOTMENT 1

Unit

I. THE CREATION 3
Feasts to Remember. The Soul of Man. The Angels.
The World. Adam and Eve. Man a Pilgrim. Doctrinal
Summary.

II. THE COMMANDMENTS 25
Feasts to Remember. Keep the Commandments. The
Ten Commandments. The Commandments of the
Church. Examination of Conscience. Doctrinal
Summary.

III. THE REDEMPTION 59
Feasts to Remember. Spiritual Crib for Christmas.
The Idea of the Redemption. The Messiah. Sugges-
tive Activities in Preparation for , Christmas. The
Baptism of Christ and the Trinity. The Crucifixion
and Resurrection. Doctrinal Summary.

IV. THE CHURCH 78
Feasts to Remember. Peter and the Power of the Keys.
The Catholic Church. The Holy Eucharist. What the
Priest Does at Mass. How Can I Be Saved. Doctrinal
Summary.

V. THE SACRAMENTS 92
Feasts to Remember. Baptism. Confession. Holy Communion. Confirmation.

FINAL REVIEW 117

The following section is an excerpt from the book "A Curriculum in Religion," included for the convenience of teachers as a way of familiarizing themselves with the basic goals laid out for the Religion in Life Curriculum for the Third Grade.

RELIGION IN GRADE III

Main Interest: Preparation for Solemn Holy Communion

THE content of the main part of the course for the third grade centers around the preparations for Holy Communion, or in the case of children who have already made the First Communion, for a better understanding of it, and a more significant spiritual life. The fundamental guide for the teacher of the grade in which the child makes his First Confession and First Communion, and of those subsequently who should stimulate regular reception of the Sacrament, are the two papal decrees on Holy Communion. For purpose of reference the text of the Decree on early Communion (Aug. 8, 1910) as related to the "age of discretion," and "the regulations" are quoted herewith.

"From all this it follows that the age of discretion required for Holy Communion is that at which the child can distinguish the Eucharistic from common and material bread and knows how to approach the altar with proper devotion.

"A perfect knowledge of the articles of faith is, therefore, not necessary. A few elements alone are sufficient. Nor is the full use of reason required, since the beginning of the use of reason, that is, some kind of reason, suffices. Wherefore to put off Communion any longer or to exact a riper age for the reception of the same is a custom that is to be rejected absolutely and the same has been repeatedly condemned by the Holy See. Thus, Pius IX, of happy memory, in the letters of Cardinal Antonelli to the Bishops of France given March 12, 1822, severely condemned the growing custom existing in some dioceses of putting off Holy Communion to a maturer age, and rejected the number of years as fixed by them.

"The S. Congregation of the Council on March 15, 1851, corrected a chapter of the Provincial Council of Rouen in which children under twelve years of age were forbidden to receive Holy Communion. This same Congregation of the Discipline of the Sacraments, acting in a similar manner in a case proposed to it from Strassburg on March 25, 1910, in which it was asked whether children of twelve or fourteen years could be admitted to Holy Communion, answered: 'Boys and girls are to be admitted to Holy Communion when they arrive at the age of discretion or attain the use of reason.'

"After seriously considering all these things, the S. Congregation of the Discipline of the Sacraments, at a general meeting held July 15, 1910, in order that the above-mentioned abuses might be removed and the children of tender years become attached to Jesus, live His life, and obtain assistance against the dangers of corruption, has judged it opportune to lay down the following:

"Norm for Admitting Children to First Holy Communion to be observed everywhere:

"1. The age of discretion required both for Confession and Communion is the time when the child begins to reason, that is about the seventh year, more or less. From this time on the obligation of satisfying the precept of both Confession and Communion begins.

"2. Both for First Confession and First Communion a complete and perfect knowledge of Christian Doctrine is not necessary. The child will, however, be obliged to learn gradually the whole Catechism according to its ability.

"3. The knowledge of Christian Doctrine required in children in order to be properly prepared for First Holy Communion is that they understand according to their capacity those mysteries of Faith which are necessary as a means of salvation, that they be able to distinguish the Eucharist from common and material bread, and also approach the sacred table with the devotion becoming their age.

"4. The obligation of the precept of Confession and Communion which rests upon the child, falls back principally upon those in whose care they are, that is, parents, confessors, teachers, and their pastor. It belongs to the father, however, or to the person taking his place, as also to the confessor, as the Roman Catechism declares, to admit the child to First Holy Communion.

"5. The pastor shall take care to announce and hold a General Communion for Children once or several times a year, and on these occasions they shall admit not only First Communicants but also others who, with the consent of their parents and the confessor, have been admitted to the sacred table before. For both classes some days of instruction and preparation shall precede.

"6. Those who have the care of children should use all diligence so that after First Communion the children shall often approach the holy table, even daily, if possible, as Jesus Christ and Mother Church desire, and that they do it with a devotion becoming their age. They should bear in mind their most important duty, by which they are obliged to have the children present at the public instructions in Catechism; otherwise they must supply this religious instruction in some other way.

"7. The custom of not admitting children to confession, or of not absolving them, is absolutely condemned. Wherefore local Ordinaries will take care that it is entirely abolished, even by using canonical punishments.

"8. It is a most intolerable abuse not to administer Viaticum and Extreme Unction to children who have attained the use of reason, and to bury them according to the manner of infants. The Ordinaries of places shall proceed severely against those who do not abandon this custom."

Outline of Main Topics

The purpose of this grade is to give the children, on their level, the general underlying conceptions of religion, or as the Decree has it: "they understand according to their capacity those mysteries of faith which are necessary as a means of salvation, that they be able to distinguish the Eucharist from common or material bread, and also approach the sacred table with the devotion becoming their age." The continuing instruction provided in this curriculum provides for the development and the knowledge acquired here.

1. God the Creator
2. Adam and Eve
3. The Sin of Adam
4. Man, a Pilgrim — Heaven His Home

5. Keep the Commandments
6. The Ten Commandments
   (1   ) I am the Lord thy God. Thou shalt not have strange gods before Me.
   (2   ) Thou shalt not take the name of the Lord thy God in vain.
   (3   ) Remember thou keep holy the Sabbath-day.
   (4   ) Honor thy father and thy mother.
   (5   ) Thou shalt not kill.
   (6, 9) Thou shalt not commit adultery.
           Thou shalt not covet thy neighbor's wife.
   (7,10) Thou shalt not steal.
           Thou shalt not covet thy neighbor's goods.
   (8   ) Thou shalt not bear false witness against thy neighbor.
7. Examination of Conscience
8. The Idea of Redemption
9. The Messiah
10. The Baptism of Christ and the Trinity
11. The Crucifixion and the Resurrection
12. The Catholic Church
13. The Holy Eucharist
14. What the Priest Does in Mass
15. How Can I Be Saved
16. Baptism
17. Peter and the Power of the Keys
18. The Confession
19. Penance
20. Method of Saying Confession
21. Holy Communion

22. The Sacrament of Confirmation
The subtopics are worked out in the syllabus.

Religious Vocabulary

Special care must be taken to see that the child's religious vocabulary is increased in connection particularly with the main topic of the grade, and that the new words are taught as the need develops and in the actual situation. Care should be taken to review words previously learned and to be sure a correct meaning is given to them on the child's own level. The words should grow in connotation as his religious knowledge and experience increases.

Words that will generally be taught in this grade are:

Blessed	commandment	Communion
Sacrament	holy	forgive
Host	Confirmation	tabernacle
loaves	Eucharist	holydays
covet	elevation	temptation
neighbor	Sunday	obligation
sacrifice		

Each teacher will be required to make up her specific lists for her specific children. No stress need be placed on the spelling of these words at present. They may be left on the board for reference.

Quotations

In this grade the quotations center around the sacrifice on Calvary, the Eucharist, and Confirmation. These are all to emphasize Christ's relation to the individual and the individual's love for Christ. Emphasis throughout is on Christ's love of children. The quotations must have their setting in relation to the more detailed discussion of the Sacrament of the Holy Eucharist which is the main interest in this grade. The quotations follow:

"Thomas answered, and said to Him: My Lord, and my God" (John xx. 28).

"This is the Bread which cometh down from heaven; that if any man eat of it, he may not die" (John vi. 50).

"I am the living Bread which came down from heaven" (John vi. 51).

"In My Father's house there are many mansions. If not, I would have told you: because I go to prepare a place for you" (John xiv. 2).

"And if I shall go, and prepare a place for you, I will come again, and will take you to Myself: that where I am, you also may be" (John xiv. 3).

"Then they laid their hands upon them, and they received the Holy Ghost" (Acts viii. 17).

"Then were little children presented to Him, that He should impose hands upon them and pray. And the disciples rebuked them.

"But Jesus said to them: 'Suffer the little children, and forbid them not to come to Me: for the kingdom of heaven is for such'" (Matt. xix. 13, 14).

"If thou wilt enter into life, keep the Commandments" (Matt. xix. 17).

(The Ten Commandments.)

"If you will not forgive men, neither will your Father forgive you" (Matt. vi. 15).

"And taking bread, He gave thanks, and brake; and gave to them, saying: 'This is My body, which is given for you. Do this for a commemoration of Me.'

"In like manner the chalice also, after He had supped, saying: 'This is the chalice, the new testament in My blood, which shall be shed for you'" (Luke xxii. 19, 20).

"If any man eat of this Bread, he shall live for ever; and the Bread that I will give, is My flesh, for the life of the world" (John vi. 52).

"And Jesus said to them: I am the Bread of life: he that cometh to Me shall not hunger: and he that believeth in Me shall never thirst" (John vi. 35).

"And he that shall receive one such little child in My name, receiveth Me" (Matt. xviii. 5).

"My little children, let us not love in word, nor in tongue, but in deed and in truth" (I John iii. 18).

"As the Father hath loved Me, I also have loved you. Abide in My love" (John xv. 9).

"All the law is fulfilled in one word: Thou shalt love thy neighbor as thyself" (Gal. v. 14).

"Jesus answered, and said to him: If any one love Me, he will keep My word, and My Father will love him, and We will come to him, and will make Our abode with him" (John xiv. 23).

"Master, which is the great commandment in the law? Jesus said to him: 'Thou shalt love the Lord thy God with thy whole heart, and with thy whole soul, and with thy whole mind.' This is the greatest and the first commandment. And the second is like to this: 'Thou shalt love thy neighbor, as thyself.' On these two commandments dependeth the whole law and the prophets" (Matt. xxii. 36–40).

"This day thou shalt be with Me in Paradise" (Luke xxiii. 43).

Pictures

The children should know the following pictures, which should be presented in connection with the stories studied. Some should be made a matter of special study:

Christ Blessing Little Children — Plockhurst
Christ Blessing Little Children — Hoffmann
Suffer Little Children to Come Unto Me — Von Uhde
Christ Blessing Little Children — Vogel
Holy Family — Defregger
Christ and the Sinner — Hoffmann
Fourth Commandment — Senkel
Christ and the Rich Young Man — Hoffmann
Prodigal Son — Molitor

Good Shepherd — Plockhurst
Divine Shepherd — Murillo
Mary Magdalene — Hoffmann
The Crucifixion — Guido Reni
The Crucifixion — Hoffmann
The Crucifixion — Munkacsy
The Miracle of the Loaves and Fishes — Murillo
The Last Supper — Da Vinci

NOTE: *The Wonder Gifts,* by Marion Ames Taggart, contains many good pictures.

Activities

The oral and written language work supplementary to the material of this grade will naturally suggest itself, as well as the paper cutting, particularly in connection with the booklets hereafter proposed. A dramatization of the Prodigal Son would be especially appropriate for this grade. The pupils in this grade will make a booklet suggested by the following: My First Communion; Jesus My Best Friend; My Prayer Book; The Commandments. All pupils might prepare the first booklet and choose one of the others or still others suggested by the teacher or the child.

The Liturgy

The child will, in this grade, get two main ideas regarding the Mass: a *general* conception of the canon of the Mass; and the relation of the Mass to the Sacrifice on Calvary. He will learn the essential words of the consecration.

Poems

The poems in this grade center for the most part about the theme of the Child's Love of God, particularly in the Blessed Sacrament. If the child has made his Communion then this material should be used to renew, reënforce and revivify his love of God in the Blessed Sacrament and in practice the regularity of reception of this Sacrament. The suggestive collection of poems for this grade are:

Nails, Leonard Feeney, S.J.
God, Father John B. Tabb
The Way of the Cross, Leonard Feeney, S.J.
Christmas Song, Lydia A. C. Ward
The Holy Baby, Father Faber
One Summer Day, Margaret E. Jordan
Raindrops, Ellen Walsh
Gates and Doors, Joyce Kilmer
A Child's Prayer, M. Betham Edwards
Morning Prayer, Monsignor Robert Hugh Benson
The Name of Mary, Adelaide A. Procter
The Christ Child, G. K. Chesterton
The Annunciation, Adelaide A. Procter
Come to Jesus, Father Faber
Spring, Mary Dixon Thayer
Autumn, Mary Dixon Thayer
First Communion Day, Faber
God's Home, E. F. Garesché, S.J.
Holy Communion, Speer Strahan
The Lamb, William Blake
Finding You, Mary Dixon Thayer
Thoughts, Mary Dixon Thayer
I Like to Think the Days Are Steps, Mary Dixon Thayer
In the Morning, Mary Dixon Thayer
Winter, Mary Dixon Thayer
The King's Highway, Rev. Hugh F. Blunt
All Things Beautiful, John Keble
A Child's Morning Prayer, Mary L. Duncan
Sleep Song, Denis A. McCarthy
Saying Grace, Robert L. Stevenson
A Child's Wish, Rev. A. J. Ryan
Oh! Heaven, I Think, Must be Alway, Father Faber
Because He Loves Us, Alice Cary

A Christmas Gift, John Francis Quinn, S.J.
A Brave Man's Hope, Katherine E. Conway
O Sacred Cross! O Holy Tree!, William Cardinal O'Connell
Holy Ghost, Come Down Upon Thy Children, Father Faber
The Blessed Trinity, Rev. F. W. Faber

Some poems are placed in the later grades to serve as a convenient opportunity to recall similar poems in the earlier grades. In a particular grade the character of the class will determine the nature of the treatment of the poem; some poems will be read by the teacher, some will be read in class, and referred to occasionally, and some will be studied with great care. For the guidance of teachers there is listed in the syllabus, the poems in previous grades which are similar to the individual poems studied in this grade.

Prayers

The more formal prayers to be taught are here listed as a basis for work in this grade. Additional prayers may be taught. The list is as follows:

1. Morning Prayers
2. Evening Prayers
3. Grace before meals
4. Grace after meals
5. Act of Contrition
6. Act of Faith
7. Act of Hope
8. Act of Charity

The "Our Father," the "Hail Mary," and the "Angelus" will be recalled to mind frequently. The "Angelus" will be said at noon.

Aspiration and Brief Prayers

As opportunity offers, the following aspirations or others will be taught. One might be selected and written on the board each month, calling attention to it as opportunity permits. The students might prepare aspirations of their own.

1. Eternal rest give unto them, O Lord, and let perpetual light shine upon them.
2. Sweet Heart of Jesus, be my love.
3. Sacred Heart of Jesus, I place my trust in Thee.
4. Lamb of God Who takest away the sins of the world, have mercy on us.
5. My Lord and my God.
6. May the Body and Blood of our Lord Jesus Christ preserve my soul to everlasting life.
7. My Jesus, mercy! Save me by Your Precious Blood.
8. Let us give thanks to the Lord, our God.
9. May the Almighty and merciful Lord grant us pardon, absolution, and remission of our sins.
10. Jesus, in the Most Holy Sacrament, have mercy on us.

Hymns

Hymns are an important factor in reënforcing the general religious instruction and training, valuable for their own content, and, if properly taught, add an element of joy to religious instruction that is quite important. The child should, at the end of instruction, know the great hymns of the Church. For the second grade there is suggested the following to be sung within the voice range of the children:

1. The Child's Prayer
2. Hymn to St. Joseph

3. A Child's Gift
4. A Child's May Hymn
5. While Shepherds Watched
6. A Child's Morning Prayer
7. The Child to the Guardian Angel
8. Jesus Teach Me How to Pray
9. O Lord, I am Not Worthy
10. Dear Angel, Ever at my Side
11. Mother Mary at Thine Altar
12. Mother, at Your Feet is Kneeling
13. Dear Guardian of Mary

Religious Practice

A definite part of the program in every grade is to build up the practice of religion in every grade and have the development cumulative throughout the grades. Wherever teachers see opportunity to build up Catholic practice they should do so. Teachers must not confound the lessons that may be essential and the actual practice in the life of the child. The pupil should understand the importance of interior disposition.

In the assignment to grade the purpose is to provide a specific time to see that the practice is established and understood. In some cases the habit will have been established. The cumulative listing of these practices is to emphasize the fact that they are not taught or established once and you are through with them. The practice must continue to be stimulated until it is "securely rooted in the life of the individual."

There should be emphasized in this grade:

1. Morning Prayer

2. Evening Prayer
3. Regular attendance at Mass on Sundays
4. Attendance at Mass on all holydays of obligation
5. Angelus
6. Bowing at the name of Jesus
7. Tipping hat or bowing as one passes church
8. Tipping hat when one meets Priest or Sister or other religious
9. Monthly Communion or more frequently

Practical Life

The translation of the religious knowledge practice and attitudes in the day-to-day life of the child must always be an objective in religious education. The elevation of the actual daily life of the individual to a supernatural plane will come about through the character of the individual's motivation. This must be a matter of development; the child must be taken, however, where he is. The lines of development are indicated but the more specific content is left for the experimentation of the first year. A teacher should always take advantage of any actual situation, and should always strive to meet difficulties which her children as a group are confronted with, no matter whether it is included in the course or not.

1. Do a good turn every day for the love of God.
   a) Daily examination of conscience at night.
   b) Daily specific review of day's thoughts, words, or deeds.
   c) Weekly complete examination of conscience for confession or as a preparation for spiritual Communion.

d) Daily expiation for the temporal punishment due to sin.

2. Cultivation of virtuous life.

3. Cultivation of school virtues.

4. Promotion of corporal and spiritual works of mercy.

Special attention is directed to the chapters on "The Christian Rule of Life" and "The Christian Daily Exercise" of the *Catechism of Christian Doctrine* approved by the Cardinal, Archbishops, and Bishops of England and Wales, and directed to be used in all their dioceses.[1]

Christian Doctrine

The formal teaching of doctrine is the main interest of the seventh and eighth grades, but that will not be the child's first contact with the doctrine. He meets it frequently at various levels, and from various angles throughout the course. He organizes this knowledge and experience in the seventh and eighth grades. We call attention here, for example, in a general way to the doctrinal content of this grade, even though the method of teaching is not the ordinary formal method.

In this grade the child receives the general groundwork of Christian doctrine: God the Father, the Creation, Adam and Eve, original sin, the commandments of God, actual sin, the Redemption, the Resurrection, the Church, the Sacrifice of the Mass, the Sacraments of Baptism, Penance (including Confession), and Confirmation.

---

[1]This is printed herewith, but is reserved for formal study in the seventh and eighth grades in the discretion of the Pastor.

As far as the creed is concerned they have the following: I believe (1) in God, the Father, (2) in Jesus Christ, His Son, (3) in the Holy Ghost, (4) in one God in three Divine Persons, (5) in the Holy Catholic Church, and (6) in the forgiveness of sins.

Basal Texts and Supplementary Material

An experimental text has been worked out for this grade called *The Life of the Soul* (Bruce). This text, besides certain fundamental information, will deal with baptism, penance, the Eucharist, and confirmation. It will include the material covered in Cardinal Gaspari's *Catechism for Children about to be Admitted to Holy Communion*. It conforms to the rule of the decree on Holy Communion of Pope Pius X. Father Kelley's *Our First Communion* (Benziger) is recommended as a supplementary text. Supplementary material will be found in:

Loyola, Mother, *First Communion*, Burns and Oates.
Loyola, Mother, *Jesus of Nazareth*, Benziger.
Sisters of Notre Dame, *First Communion Day*, Herder.
Eaton, Mary, *The Little Ones*, Herder.
Brownson, J. Van Dyke, *To the Heart of a Child*, Universal Knowledge Foundation.
Matimore, Rev. P. Henry, *A Child's Garden of Religious Stories*, pp. 243–260, Macmillan.
Sisters of Notre Dame, *Thoughts and Prayers for First Communion*, Herder.
Taggart, Marion Ames, *The Wonder Gifts*, Benziger.
Sisters of St. Dominic, *My Gift to Jesus*, Lawdale.
de Zulueta, Rev. F. M., *Child Prepared for First Communion*, Benziger.
Eleanore, Sister M., *The Little Flower's Love for the Holy Eucharist*, Benziger.

EXCERPTS FROM

The Christian's Rule of Life

I

What Rule of Life Must We Follow if We Hope to be Saved?

If we hope to be saved, we must follow the rule of life taught by Jesus Christ.

What Are We Bound to Do by the Rule of Life Taught by Jesus Christ?

By the rule of life taught by Jesus Christ we are bound always to hate sin and to love God.

How Must We Hate Sin?

We must hate sin above all other evils, so as to be resolved never to commit a willful sin, for the love or fear of anything whatsoever.

How Must We Love God?

We must love God above all things, and with our whole heart.

How Must We Learn to Love God?

We must learn to love God by begging of God to teach us to love Him: "O my God, teach me to love Thee."

II

What Will the Love of God Lead Us to Do?

The love of God will lead us often to think how good God is; often to speak to Him in our hearts and always to seek to please Him.

Does Jesus Christ Also Command Us to Love One Another?

Jesus Christ also commands us to love one another — that is, all persons, without exception — for His sake.

How Are We to Love One Another?

We are to love one another by wishing well to one another, and praying for one another; and by never allowing ourselves any thought, word, or deed to the injury of anyone.

Are We Also Bound to Love Our Enemies?

We are also bound to love our enemies, not only by forgiving them from our hearts, but also by wishing them well, and praying for them.

Has Jesus Christ Given Us Another Great Rule?

Jesus Christ has given us another great rule in these words: "If any man will come after Me, let him deny himself, and take up his cross daily, and follow Me" (Luke ix. 23).

How Are We to Deny Ourselves?

We are to deny ourselves by giving up our own will, and by going against our own humors, inclinations, and passions.

Why Are We Bound to Deny Ourselves?

We are bound to deny ourselves because our natural inclinations are prone to evil from our very childhood; and, if not corrected by self-denial, they will certainly carry us to hell.

How Are We to Take Up Our Cross Daily?

We are to take up our cross daily by submitting daily with patience to the labors and sufferings of this short life, and by bearing them willingly for the love of God.

III

How Are We to Follow Our Blessed Lord?

We are to follow our Blessed Lord by walking in His footsteps and imitating His virtues.

What Are the Principal Virtues We Are to Learn of Our Blessed Lord?

The principal virtues we are to learn of our Blessed Lord are: meekness, humility, and obedience.

Which Are the Enemies We Must Fight Against All the Days of Our Life?

The enemies which we must fight against all the days of our life are: the devil, the world, and the flesh.

What Do You Mean by the Devil?

By the devil I mean Satan and all his wicked angels, who are ever seeking to draw us into sin, that we may be damned with them.

What Do You Mean by the World?

By the world I mean the false maxims of the world, and the society of those who love the vanities, riches, and pleasures of this world better than God.

Why Do You Number the Devil and the World Among the Enemies of the Soul?

I number the devil and the world among the enemies of the soul because they are always seeking by temptation, and by word or example, to carry us along with them in the broad road that leads to damnation.

What Do You Mean by the Flesh?

By the flesh, I mean our own corrupt inclinations and passions, which are the most dangerous of all our enemies.

What Must We Do to Hinder the Enemies of Our Soul from Drawing Us Into Sin?

To hinder the enemies of our soul from drawing us into sin, we must watch, pray, and fight against all their suggestions and temptations.

In the Warfare Against the Devil, the World, and the Flesh on Whom Must We Depend?

In the warfare against the devil, the world, and the flesh we must depend, not on ourselves, but on God only: "I can do all things in Him Who strengtheneth me" (Phil. iv. 13).

IV

The Christian's Daily Exercise

How Should You Begin the Day?

I should begin the day by making the Sign of the Cross as soon as I awake in the morning, and by saying some short prayer, such as: "O my God, I offer my heart and soul to Thee."

How Should You Rise in the Morning?

I should rise in the morning diligently, dress myself modestly, and then kneel down and say my morning prayers.

Should You Also Hear Mass if You Have Time and Opportunity?

I should also hear Mass if I have time and opportunity, for to hear Mass is by far the best and most profitable of all devotions.

Is It Useful to Make Daily Meditation?

It is useful to make daily meditation, for such was the practice of all the saints.

On What Ought We to Meditate?

We ought to meditate especially on the four last things, and the life and passion of our Blessed Lord.

Ought We Frequently to Read Good Books?

We ought frequently to read good books, such as the Holy Gospels, the Lives of the Saints, and other spiritual works, which nourish our faith and piety, and arm us against the false maxims of the world.

And What Should You Do as to Your Eating, Drinking, Sleeping, and Amusements?

As to my eating, drinking, sleeping, and amusements, I should use all these things with moderation, and with a desire to please God.

Say the Grace Before Meals.

"Bless us, O Lord, and these Thy gifts, which we are going to receive from Thy bounty, through Christ our Lord. Amen."

Say Grace After Meals.

"We give Thee thanks, Almighty God, for all Thy benefits, Who livest and reignest, world without end. Amen. May the souls of the faithful departed, through the mercy of God, rest in peace. Amen."

How Should You Sanctify Your Ordinary Actions and Employments of the Day?

I should sanctify my ordinary actions and employments of the day by often raising up my heart to God whilst I am about them, and saying some short prayer to Him.

What Should You do When You Find Yourself Tempted to Sin?

When I find myself tempted to sin I should make the Sign of the Cross on my heart, and call on God as earnestly as I can, saying "Lord, save me, or I perish."

If You Have Fallen Into Sin, What Should You Do?

If I have fallen into sin, I should cast myself in spirit at the feet of Christ, and humbly beg His pardon by a sincere act of contrition.

When God Sends You Any Cross, or Sickness, or Pain, What Should You Say?

When God sends me any cross, or sickness, or pain, I should say, "Lord, Thy will be done; I take this for my sins."

What Little Indulgenced Prayers Would You do Well to Say Often to Yourself During the Day?

I should do well to say often to myself during the day such little indulgenced prayers as:

"Glory be to the Father, and to the Son, and to the Holy Ghost; as it was in the beginning, is now, and ever shall be, world without end. Amen."

"In all things may the most holy, the most just, and the most lovable will of God be done, praised, and exalted above all for ever."

"O Sacrament most holy, O Sacrament, Divine, all praise and all thanksgiving be every moment Thine."

"Praised be Jesus Christ, praised for evermore."

"My Jesus, mercy; Mary, help."

How Should You Finish the Day?

I should finish the day by kneeling down and saying my night prayers.

After Your Night Prayers What Should You Do?

After my night prayers I should observe due modesty in going to bed; occupy myself with the thoughts of death; and endeavor to compose myself to rest at the foot of the cross, and give my last thoughts to my crucified Savior.

RELIGION IN GRADE III

SUGGESTIONS FOR THE TEACHER

Time Allotment

The time for each lesson in the Religion Course is approximately one week. The teacher is, however, not strictly bound to hold to this order week for week. If she finds that one lesson requires more than the specified time, or that another has been unduly prolonged, she is at liberty tò make the desired change. She should, in that case, however, make a note of the change under Teachers' Notes together with her recommendations for suggested changes.

The Textbook

In connection with each lesson from the text, there is given a suggestive series of questions or a series of sentences with certain words omitted to be filled in by the student.

These questions or sentences with blanks to be filled in may be used in connection with the text in various ways:

1. With textbook open, the pupils themselves find the answers to the question, or the correct word for the blank.

2. These questions or blanks may be used in anticipation of the lesson to guide the reading.

3. They may be used as a test after the lesson has been mastered.

4. They may be used as a review on succeeding days.

5. They should be used as a review prior to the study of the Christian Doctrine summary.

The teacher should check in this manual the way she uses the textbook, and note under Teachers' Notes the effectiveness of the method used.

Vocabulary

There are listed under this heading in each lesson from the text only the words of religious significance or associated with

Scriptural stories. These words are listed ordinarily the first time they appear. Many of them have been studied in previous grades; these will be reviewed. The others will be studied as new ones. Generous provision is always made for subsequent repetition of the common words in later lessons.

Pictures

By all means the teacher should use as many pictures as possible in connection with the daily lesson. Generally they serve as an approach to the new lesson: but they should be kept before the children during the entire week, in a convenient place and at a height well within the pupils' vision. The children should be allowed to examine and talk about them, not only during the religion period, but at any time during the day when the opportunity presents itself. A picture may at times serve as a basis for a review or for correlated work in oral or written language, spelling, number work, and so on.

The pictures presented to the children should be Catholic in conception and, if possible, attractively colored. It would be well for the teacher to keep separate files for the collection of pictures pertaining to each lesson. Children could also be interested in adding to the collection. Incidentally, such an activity on their part would help to stimulate the imagination, to impress religious truths more deeply, and to apply the lessons learned at school to life situations.

The Story

The wording of the stories as given in the plan is merely suggestive. It is understood that the teacher is not to use the story *verbatim,* but rather that she adapt her language to the comprehension of the children as far as she can. When necessary, she will explain the meaning of unusual words, or in some cases bring home their significance by means of some simple activity.

The teacher should be careful not to overemphasize the purely imaginative details of the story, but keep close to the simple, scriptural narrative. That does not necessarily mean that the story must be devoid of all interest and imaginative coloring. On the contrary, the religion period should bring with it an atmosphere of spiritual warmth, or reverence, wonder, and joy.

Doctrine

The stories developed from week to week contain in themselves all the religious instructions necessary for the first four grades. The review following the lesson merely indicates the possible range of truths that may be gleaned from a particular story. The formal teaching of doctrine in grades 1, 2, 3, and 4, that is, through routine questions and answers is not an essential part of the plan. It is a by-product. It must not be assumed, therefore, that it is not effectively done — even more effectively than if it were directly aimed at. It may be well to note here what Father F. H. Drinkwater says in this connection in his Introduction to Tahon's *The First Instruction of Children and Beginners*, pp. 18–19.

"It is asserted that without a fixed form of words, teachers, whether good or bad, will just flounder about vaguely, with no pegs on which to hang their doctrine, so that the children in the end will retain nothing definite at all. This is quite true, of course, but it is not a reason for teaching the answers of the Catechism to young children; it is only a reason why the teacher should often crystallize his teaching into little fixed phrases and sentences which the children will take in and remember. Any tolerable class teacher of young children will soon evolve with them a temporary Catechism of their own, in their own language, and as definite and well-memorized as anybody could wish; but there is all the difference in the world between a living catechesis of that kind, created out of the mental contact of this particular teacher with these particular children, and the process of forcibly feeding children with the official Catechism intended for the grown-up laity; more especially when that process is urged on by regular visits of an outside examiner." This living catechesis may, and in most cases will, result in the formulation of religious truth as given in the *Baltimore Catechism*. But after such a procedure as is here definitely indicated, it will no longer be inert and dead, but living and effective.

Poems, Hymns, Quotations

The teacher should have at her disposal a collection of suitable poems, hymns, and quotations gathered from year to year for use in the religion class. Some of the simpler poems suggested in the course should be memorized by the children. Other poems may be substituted in their place if the teacher so desires. Scriptural quotations must be explained to the children or directly tied up with an activity that will make the meaning clear to them.

The poems, hymns, and quotations memorized by the children may serve as prayers for various occasions, especially before and after Holy Communion: Such as the hymn,

"Jesus, Jesus, come to me
Oh, how much I long for Thee."

Some of the poems are intended for reading by the teacher only, and may at times be used as an introduction to the day's lesson or as a review of former lessons. Not all need necessarily be of a strictly religious nature, provided they serve otherwise to bring home the truth aimed at.

Hymns should be taught during the singing period. They, as well as the poems and quotations, should be correlated with other subjects of the day.

Practical Life

The little hints for practical life, referred to in the daily or weekly lesson, are usually suggested by some person or event connected with the story. As it is remarked in the outline of this course, "A teacher should always take advantage of any actual situation and should always strive to meet difficulties with which her children as a group are confronted, no matter whether it is included in the course or not." It would be well at times to have the pupils suggest their own little practices, always simple and specific, and to check up on them later. The religious motive for such acts should be kept before them and discussed with them occasionally. Other practices may be added, the teacher being careful, however, to keep to a few simple acts well motivated, rather than a great variety performed in a mechanical way.

Activities

The chief purpose of the activities suggested in connection with the religion story, is to furnish assimilative material and to associate the lesson as far as possible with everyday experiences. The teacher is not bound to carry out all these activities in accordance with the plan. They are merely suggestive. She may substitute, add to, or change them as her own experience may prompt. One thing, however, she must keep in mind, and that is, that the activities are supplementary and serve to bring out more clearly or to review the lesson of the week.

They are a means to an end and should not be made an end in themselves. It would be a mistake, for example, to work out an elaborate project on the sand table and then lose sight of the purpose for which it was undertaken. To obviate any such difficulty, the teacher should often have the children tell the story as they build up the project and should review by careful questioning the underlying lesson. The activities suggested under the heading "Development" are varied from lesson to lesson merely to suggest different ways in which the work may be made more interesting. Naturally such exercises as oral and written language work could and should be used frequently in connection with the religion lesson.

Pupils' Readings

The selected readings are taken from Catholic Readers of the particular grade in question. It would be a valuable contribution to the spiritual and intellectual life of the children, if there could be placed somewhere within their reach, preferably at a separate table in their own classroom, all the available religious books adapted to their age, for them to read and handle as time and circumstances allow. The children will find great pleasure in selecting their own pictures, stories, or even words connected with the lesson, and should not be denied the privilege of some such task, no matter how small it may be. A list of religious books together with their price is appended.

Teacher's Notes

The space left for the teacher's notes should be well utilized. In it should be noted any improvements, criticisms, or suggestions that might be helpful either for the teacher herself or for a revision of the plan. It should also contain information as to the sources of helpful material used, such as poems, texts, pictures, and as to activities and practices that proved unusually successful. Pupil reactions and suggestions should also be noted.

General

Pupils should be encouraged again and again, after the first few weeks are over, to show the results of their efforts to their parents, to tell their little stories to them, to get them to pray with them, to go to Holy Communion with them. No parents can long resist the pleadings of a little one; indeed, many a careless Catholic has been brought back to the Church through the innocent remarks of a child.

The lesson in religion should never be a thing apart from the rest of the day's activities. If it is whole-heartedly entered into, if it has become part of the very life of the teacher and child, then it must of necessity permeate every action of the day. That does not necessarily mean that all the day's work must be work in religion, but rather that religion lends color and interest to all the actions of the day.

The more important feasts of the ecclesiastical year should be dwelt on as they occur.

After all is said and done, the teacher is and always must be the most important factor in the teaching of religion. And the more she realizes her exalted position, the more conscientious will she be in preparing herself for the great work of leading the little ones ever closer to the Heart of God.

RELIGION COURSE—GRADE THREE

Time Allotment[1]

SEPTEMBER

First Week — Soul of Man
Reading, *The Life of the Soul*
Lessons 1, 2, and 3

Second Week — The Soul of Man (Angels, optional or condensed)

Third Week — The World

Fourth Week — Adam and Eve

OCTOBER

First Week — Man a Pilgrim

Second Week — Keep the Commandments
The Ten Commandments

Third Week — The First Commandment

Fourth Week — The Second Commandment

NOVEMBER

First Week — The Third Commandment

Second Week — The Fourth Commandment

Third Week — The Fifth Commandment

Fourth Week — Sixth and Ninth Commandments

DECEMBER

First Week — Seventh and Tenth Commandments

Second and Third Weeks — The Idea of Redemption
The Messiah

JANUARY

First Week — The Messiah

Second Week — The Messiah

Third Week — The Eighth Commandment

---

[1]This is merely suggestive. The teacher's supplementary enrichment as provided in this manual makes it possible to extend or reduce the time assignments. In every case it is not expected that all the proposals under the heading "Development," will be followed. But the suggestions make possible an adaptation of the work to the varying abilities of classes.

Fourth Week — Review of the Ten Commandments
The Commandments of the Church

FEBRUARY

First Week — Examination of Conscience

Second Week — Baptism of Christ and the Trinity

Third Week — The Crucifixion and Resurrection

Fourth Week — The Crucifixion and Resurrection

MARCH

First Week — The Crucifixion and Resurrection

Second Week — Peter and the Power of the Keys
The Church

Third and Fourth Weeks — The Holy Eucharist
What the Priest Does at Mass

APRIL

First Week — How Can I be Saved

Second Week — Baptism

Third Week — Confession

Fourth Week — Confession

MAY

First Week — Holy Communion

Second Week — Holy Communion

Third Week — Holy Communion

Fourth Week — Holy Communion

JUNE

First Week — Confirmation

Second Week — Review

UNIT I
THE CREATION

Time: Second week in September to the first week in October, inclusive.

    I. The Soul of Man.
    Ia. The Angels (Optional).
    II. The World.
    III. Adam and Eve.
    IV. Man a Pilgrim.

Feasts to Remember

September 8, Nativity of the Blessed Virgin Mary
September 12, Holy Name of Mary
September 15, Seven Dolors of the Blessed Virgin Mary
September 29, St. Michael
October 2, Holy Guardian Angel

I. The Soul of Man

Presentation. The teacher will ask, What is the name of our new book? Have you a soul? Has Jane a soul? Has Robert a soul? Has Francis a soul? Yes. Every human being has a soul. We know we have a body and a soul.

The teacher will encourage the students to talk about the soul. How very real and active it is, even though we do not see it. How it loves. How it is sorry. How it makes mistakes sometimes. How it is naughty. The emphasis should be on the beauty and loveliness of the soul — and its very great importance.

It is the purpose of this book among other things to make the "soul" an active part of the students' vocabulary and thought, and to make the child soul-conscious. The ultimate purpose is to make the child realize that there is a *life of the soul.* The

3

teacher will recur to this frequently throughout the year. The beginning is to be in this first lesson.

Mottoes and Posters. For blackboard mottoes and posters the following are suggested:

Man is a body and soul.

It is the soul of man that is like God.

God is Love. Love God.

The soul is more important than the body.

Pictures for study.

Pictures of people of different nationalities.

Pictures of children engaged in various activities.

Pictures of children or old persons doing kind or other good acts.

Development:

1. In the oral conversation about the soul, and how it directs, the teacher will, of course, use frequently the words in the first three lessons as given below, and any others that may be necessary.

2. Have the children write a series of sentences about "My Soul." This might be continued as a "My Soul" booklet. Some typical sentences might be:

I have a soul.

My soul made me get up early this morning when I wanted to stay in bed.

My soul tells me to obey my mother and father.

My soul says to me: "Love God."

God was good to give me a soul and body.

3. Associate pictures of good acts with the activity of the soul. If the discussion brings it out, of course, tell the children the soul may do bad things as well as good.

4. Make a list of good acts your soul did in one day or one week. The teacher will read them to the class without naming the child except for some very good reason.

5. For a review, point out how you must take care of your body. Show, too, or have the child suggest, that you must take care of your soul.

6. Tell or read some simple stories about good children, which give opportunity to emphasize the importance of the soul.

7. Study the poem "Little Drops of Water," by Julia A. F. Carney, with special emphasis on the fourth stanza.

8. Have children write simple prayers:

My soul loves God.

I love God.

I am thankful to God for my soul.

The Text:

Read Lesson 1, *The Life of the Soul.*

The text will be used in this lesson as:[1]

1. Introduction to the lesson.
2. Development of the lesson.
3. Summary of the lesson.
4. Review of the lesson.

Content: The particular content of this lesson will be found by pupils finding out answers to the following questions or answering in the blank spaces the correct words:

Of what is man composed?

What does the soul tell the hands? What do they do?

What does the soul tell the legs? What do they do?

What does the soul tell the ears? What do they do?

What does the soul tell the eyes? What do they do?

What does the soul tell the mouth? What does it do?

The body obeys the . . . .

Soul and . . . . must work together.

Is the soul always good?

God wants body and soul to work together in order to go to . . . .

Which is more important, soul or body? Why?

What are we going to learn in this book?

The Text:

Read Lesson 2, *The Life of the Soul.*

The text will be used in this lesson as:

1. Introduction to the lesson.

---

[1] Check how you use the text and note under Teachers' Notes the effectiveness of this note.

2. Development of the lesson.
3. Summary of the lesson.
4. Review of the lesson.

Content: The particular content of this lesson will be found by pupils finding out answers to the following questions, or answering in the blank spaces the correct words:

God created .... :
God created all ....
God made man to His .... and ....
God made man and ....
God gave man power over all ....
God told man to rule over all ....
What book tells us these things?

The Text:

Read Lesson 3, *The Life of the Soul.*
The text will be used in this lesson as:
1. Introduction to the lesson.
2. Development of the lesson.
3. Summary of the lesson.
4. Review of the lesson.

Content: The particular content of this lesson will be found by pupils answering in the blank spaces the correct words:

God made ....
God made man's ....
God made man's ....
Man is composed of .... and ....
Man's soul is like ....
Man has a living ....
.... is a spirit.
My .... is a spirit.

The Text:

Read Lesson 4, *The Life of the Soul.*
The text will be used in this lesson as:
1. Introduction to the lesson.
2. Development of the lesson.
3. Summary of the lesson.
4. Review of the lesson.

Content: The particular content of this lesson will be found by pupils answering in the blank spaces the correct words:

Did anything live before God?

God lived before the ....

God lived before the ...., the moon, and the .... were made.

God had no ....

God has no ....

The soul has a ....

The soul has no ....

I love ....

.... loves me.

.... is a spirit.

God is a pure ....

God is a spirit perfect in .... way.

God is a spirit infinitely ....

Vocabulary: This vocabulary includes the words with religious content or associated with Scriptural narratives:

Lesson 1: composed; soul; God; created; heaven.

Lesson 2: creation; likeness; Bible; image.

Lesson 3: slime; spirit; living soul.

Lesson 4: eternal; infinitely; perfect.

Development:

1. A different group of children may be appointed each week to choose and prepare the posters or mottoes for the lesson. Their own reader, *The Life of the Soul,* will offer the best suggestions for the purpose.

2. Teach the poem "Angels," by M. D. Thayer, or another appropriate angel poem.

3. Art pictures to select from:

Guardian Angel — Hofmann

Guardian Angel — Guercian

Guardian Angel — Murillo

4. It would be well to have on hand some of the pictures such as *Expulsion from Paradise, The Annunciation, Shepherds,* and others referring to the stories, and have the children talk about them.

Take this occasion to review the Angelus and illustrate the different scenes by pictures. Let the children say the Angelus while the pictures are being shown.

5. Show the picture of *St. Michael,* by Raphael, if it is available and have the children talk about it.

6. Dramatize the Guardian Angel watching over a group of children. The class may sing an angel hymn during this time, recite a poem, or the Scripture text "He hath given His angels charge over thee."

7. Show the *Angelus,* by Millet, and let the pupils write a few sentences about it.

8. For oral language work have the children find stories about angels in supplementary readers and tell them to the class.

9. Written language exercise: Write five sentences about the angels. What new words have you learned in this lesson? Use them in sentences.

10. Related poems and stories from different sources should be used for appreciation and supplementary reading.

Pupils' Readings:

Standard Catholic Reader, III, p. 65, "The Sunbeam," Tabb.

Ideal, III, p. 54, "Hush, My Dear, Be Still and Slumber."

Every Child's Garden, p. 11, "The Sin of the Angels"; p. 12, "The Bad Angels."

Teachers' References:

The Holy Bible, Ps. xc. 11; Matt. iv. 16.

The Little Ones, "The Angels," pp. 16–25.

Practical Aids, "The Smile of Your Guardian Angel," p. 13; "Help of the Guardian Angel," p. 79; "Protected by an Angel," p. 146.

To the Heart of the Child, Lesson III, "The Angels."

Teacher Tells a Story, Vol. I, pp. 79–80.

Catholic School Journal, October, 1931.

Teachers' Notes:

(Ia) The Angels
Optional

The week's work is a review of the lesson on angels and takes the form of a variety of activities.

The "Development" following this and future lessons suggests a number of these activities, any of which may be used by the teacher.

Keep before the children, by means of posters or blackboard mottoes, such thoughts as the following:

God made me.
God sees me.
God loves me.
My Angel watches over me.

(See Developments 1 and 2.)

Teach or review a hymn, such as the following:

Dear Angel, Ever at my Side.
The Child to the Guardian Angel.

Pictures:

Use the picture *The Guardian Angel* (Plockhorst) or some other angel picture. For other appropriate art pictures see Development 3.

Review:

Who made the angels? Where are the angels? Can we see them? Why not? What do the angels do in heaven? What do they do for us?

Presentation:

Relate the story of the creation and fall of the angels.

Have the children recall various occasions when angels appeared to men and let them tell the stories to the class. (See Development 4.)

Dwell particularly on God's hatred of evil. He punished the wicked angels by sending them into hell. They are jealous of us and try to lead us into sin. (See Development 5.)

Instill a deep love for the Guardian Angel. Our angel loves us and helps us to be good. (See Development 6.)

Read Lesson 4 in *The Life of the Soul*.

For further activities see Developments 7, 8, 9, and 10.

II. The World

Stress frequently during this week the all-important thought: "God made me. I belong to God. God wants me to be happy with Him in heaven." Repeat this idea time and again in connection with future lessons.

For posters or blackboard mottoes some of the following may be used:

God made the flowers.

God made the birds.

A gift of God (picture of fruits or flowers).

I believe in God the Father, Creator of heaven and earth.

Teach the poem "All Things Beautiful," by Keble. (See Development 1.)

Pictures:

The Creation of Animals — Paola

Different nature scenes with sun, moon, stars, plants, animals, etc.

Review:

Who made the angels? Why did God make them? Who made the earth? The sky, the water, the light? How did God make all these things? God said: "Let there be light" and there was light. For whom did God make all these things? How can we show our gratitude to God? (See Development 2.)

Presentation:

Review the different days of creation as given in the Bible History. Have the children point out on the pictures what God created on the different days and tell the particular purpose for which each creature was made. (See Developments 3 and 4.)

Read and discuss Lessons 5 and 6 in *The Life of the Soul*.

Other activities are suggested in Developments 5 and 6.

The Text:

Read Lesson 5, *The Life of the Soul* (God Made Man).

The text will be used in this lesson as:

1. Introduction to the lesson.

2. Development of the lesson.
3. Summary of the lesson.
4. Review of the lesson.

Content: The particular content of this lesson will be found by pupils answering in the blank spaces the correct words:

God made me to .... Him.

God made me to .... Him.

God made me to .... Him.

.... love God.

.... love my neighbor, because God made him too.

.... love all God's creatures.

God wants me to be happy with Him in ....

The Text:

Read Lesson 6, *The Life of the Soul* (God the Father).

The text will be used in this lesson as:

1. Introduction to the lesson.
2. Development of the lesson.
3. Summary of the lesson.
4. Review of the lesson.

Content: The particular content of this lesson will be found by pupils finding out answers to the following questions, or answering in the blank spaces the correct words:

God made the ....

God made the ....

God made all ....

Who made you?

Who made me?

We are His ....

.... is our Father.

Who taught us to call God our Father?

.... believe in God, the Father Almighty.

.... believe in God, the Creator of heaven and earth and all things.

Vocabulary: This vocabulary includes the words with religious content or associated with Scriptural narratives:

Lesson 5: neighbor; forever; service; heavenly.

Lesson 6: heavens; Christ; almighty; Creator; believe.

Development:

1. Other poems for study or reading:

"Rainbows" — Ellen Walsh

"God" — Father Tabb

"All Things Beautiful" — John Keble

"The Wonderful World"

"Creation" — Berdice Moran

"Thanksgiving" — Mary Dixon Thayer

"Father in Heaven, We Thank Thee" — Anon.

2. Read to the children "How God Made the World," *A Child's Garden of Religious Stories,* Chapter 1, and have them repeat parts of the story for oral language work.

3. Have the children make a chart for different days of creation, one for each day, by pasting pictures of the various things created on large sheets of paper, as the story progresses.

4. Encourage creative work in clay modeling, paper cutting, drawing, or poster making, of the different creatures of God. Have the children repeat often while they are at work: "God made the flowers," "God made the trees," "Thank You, dear God."

5. Let the pupils tell stories of the creation they have read in other readers.

6. Make a sand-table project of the creation.

7. Study the pictures in *The Life of the Soul* on Creation (p. 8).

8. By reference to Holy Scripture as given below, the teacher will tell the story in which the following text appeared so that the child will understand it in its setting:

"In the beginning God created heaven and earth.

And the earth was void and empty, and darkness was upon the face of the deep; and the spirit of God moved over the waters.

And God said: Be light made. And light was made,

And God saw the light that it was good; and He divided the light from the darkness" (Gen. i. 1–4).

The children will memorize the text.

Pupils' Readings:

Every Child's Garden, p. 14, "God Made all Things."

Ideal Catholic Reader, III, p. 80, "The Creation"; p. 83, "Children, Thank God"; p. 104, "The Garden of Eden"; p. 30, "The Reason Why."

American Cardinal, p. 216, "God's Outdoors."

Teachers' References:

The Holy Bible, Book of Genesis.

Our Little Ones, p. 14, "God Made Everything"; p. 59, "Adam and Eve"; p. 53, "God's Power."

Teachers' Notes:

III. Adam and Eve

As an introduction to this lesson have the pupils read Lesson 7 in *The Life of the Soul.*

For blackboard mottoes and posters the following are suggested:

"Dust thou art and into dust thou shalt return."

Disobedience always makes us unhappy (picture of children punished).

I must obey my parents.

Teach or review a hymn to the Blessed Virgin, Mother of the promised Redeemer. (See Development 1.)

Pictures:

Expulsion of Adam and Eve from the Garden — Doré

Madonna — Bodenhausen, or

Immaculate Conception — Murillo

Review:

What did God create on the sixth day? How did God create Adam? How did God make Eve? Were Adam and Eve happy in Paradise? Did they always remain happy? Why not? Who can tell me what happened to Adam and Eve?

Presentation:

Relate or have the children read the following stories:

Adam and Eve in Paradise.

The Temptation and Fall. (See Development 2.)

The Punishment.

The Promise of the Redeemer. (See Development 5.)

Stress the fact that through the sin of our first parents, heaven was closed and death and sorrow came into the world. All the sorrow in the world came because of the sin of our first parents. If they had kept God's command, we too, should always have been good and happy.

God made Adam and Eve for heaven. Because they were disobedient heaven was closed. God also made us for heaven. God is just and therefore must punish sin; but He is also merciful. He promised a Redeemer. Disobedience always makes us unhappy. (See Developments 3 and 4.)

Read Lessons 8 and 9 in *The Life of the Soul.*

For further activities see Developments 6, 7, and 8.

The Text:

Read Lesson 7, *The Life of the Soul* (Man in Paradise).

The text will be used in this lesson as:

1. Introduction to the lesson.
2. Development of the lesson.
3. Summary of the lesson.
4. Review of the lesson.

Content: The particular content of this lesson will be found by pupils answering in the blank spaces the correct words:

Paradise was a .... place.

Paradise was a .... park.

Paradise was a .... garden.

Paradise had all .... of trees.

In Paradise was the Tree of ....

In Paradise was the Tree of ....

Tell how beautiful and wonderful Paradise was.

The Text:

Read Lesson 8, *The Life of the Soul* (God's Command to Adam).

The text will be used in this lesson as:

1. Introduction to the lesson.
2. Development of the lesson.
3. Summary of the lesson.
4. Review of the lesson.

Content: The particular content of this lesson will be found by pupils finding out answers to the following questions:

What was God's command to Adam?

What would happen to Adam if he did not keep God's commandment?

Would you have kept God's command?

The Text:

Read Lesson 9, *The Life of the Soul* (God Creates Eve).

The text will be used in this lesson as:

1. Introduction to the lesson.
2. Development of the lesson.
3. Summary of the lesson.
4. Review of the lesson.

Content: The particular content of this lesson will be found by pupils finding out answers to the following questions or answering in the blank spaces the correct words:

Who said,

"Let Us make him a helper like himself"?

"She is bone of my bone. She is flesh of my flesh"?

To whom?

How was Eve made?

Man and wife are .... flesh.

The Text:

Read Lesson 10, *The Life of the Soul* (Adam Disobeys God).

The text will be used in this lesson as:

1. Introduction to the lesson.
2. Development of the lesson.
3. Summary of the lesson.
4. Review of the lesson.

Content: The particular content of this lesson will be found by pupils finding out answers to the following questions or answering in the blank spaces the correct words:

Who said, "Of every tree in Paradise thou shalt eat, but thou shalt not eat of the Tree of Knowledge"? (Lesson 8.)

To whom was it said?

Who said, "You shall not die if you eat of the Tree of Knowledge"?

To whom was it said?

Who said, "You shall be as God, knowing good and knowing evil"?

To whom was it said?

Adam was forbidden to eat of the Tree of ....

Whom did the devil tempt?

What promise did he make?

Eve ate the forbidden fruit of the .... of ....

Eve gave .... the fruit of the tree.

Adam ...., too.

Did Adam sin? Why?

When do we sin?

The Text:

Read Lesson 11, *The Life of the Soul* (Adam is punished).

The text will be used in this lesson as:

1. Introduction to the lesson.
2. Development of the lesson.
3. Summary of the lesson.
4. Review of the lesson.

Content: The particular content of this lesson will be found by pupils answering in the blank spaces the correct words; or finding out answers to the following questions:

Who said, "Thou shalt eat the earth all the days of thy life"?

To whom was it said?

Who said, "In the sweat of thy face shalt thou eat bread"?

To whom was it said?

Who said, "For dust thou art, and into dust thou shalt return"?

To whom was it said?

God knew the devil tempted ....

God knew Eve tempted . . . .
What was the punishment of the serpent?
What was the punishment of Eve?
What was the punishment of Adam?
What promise was made by God?
Who is the Savior of men?

The Text:

Read Lesson 12, *The Life of the Soul* (Grace, the Life of the Soul).

The text will be used in this lesson as:

1. Introduction to the lesson.
2. Development of the lesson.
3. Summary of the lesson.
4. Review of the lesson.

Content: The particular content of this lesson will be found by pupils finding out answers to the following questions or answering in the blank spaces the correct words:

. . . . is the life of the soul.

Name three things about the soul of Adam before his disobedience.

What happened to Adam's soul because of his disobedience?

What is true of the soul of all persons who are born?

The lack of grace in our soul at birth is called . . . . sin.

We are born without . . . . in our soul.

We are born in original . . . .

We can secure . . . . easily.

This is possible through . . . . our Redeemer.

In this way the promise to . . . . was kept.

Vocabulary: This vocabulary includes the words with religious content or associated with Scriptural narratives:

Lesson 7: Paradise; Tree of Life; Tree of Knowledge; Adam.

Lesson 8: forbade.

Lesson 9: Eve.

Lesson 10: disobeys; sinned; serpent; disguised; sin; evil; good; devil.

Lesson 11: punished; disobedience; Redeemer; dust; sweat; Savior; glorious.

Lesson 12: grace; law; original; sanctifying; will; Jesus; holy; sanctifies.

Development:

1. Hymns which may be taught:

    Mother Mary at Thine Altar

    Mother at Your Feet is Kneeling

2. Have pupils find a story about someone being tempted. Discuss temptation with them and avoidance of occasions of sin, such as bad companions. Teach the use of prayer in temptation.

3. Talk about heaven and all it holds for us. See *Our Little Ones,* p. 74.

4. Show how heaven is lost by sin and how it can be regained. Review the Act of Contrition and impress upon the children the various occasions on which it is important to make an Act of Contrition: after committing sin; before going to bed; before confession; when there is to be danger of death either for themselves or for those with whom they happen to be. Some children have had experiences of danger or seen serious accidents. Let them tell the class about it.

5. Show a picture of the Blessed Mother with her child in her arms. Also one of the Christ Child or the Birth of Christ. If time permits let them talk about these pictures in reference to the promised Redeemer.

6. Dramatization: Have the pupils select a group to represent Adam, Eve, and their children. Adam and Eve take turns in describing Paradise in all its beauty. The children occasionally ask questions.

Have another group tell of the Temptation and Fall and still another of the Punishment and the Promised Redeemer. Give the children a chance to show their own ingenuity and encourage them here and elsewhere to use the simpler scripture texts, especially, "Remember, man, that thou art dust . . ." in connection with their work.

7. Poems for study or reading:

Every Child's Garden, "Our First Parents," p. 17; "Original Sin," p. 18; "Temptation," p. 19; "After the Sin," p. 20; "The Punishment Begins," p. 21.

"The Name of Mary" — Adelaide Proctor.

"Autumn" — M. D. Thayer.

8. From Lesson 7 in *The Life of the Soul* let the children describe Paradise as they picture it. Have them make a drawing or sand-table illustration of Paradise.

9. By reference to Holy Scripture as given below, the teacher will tell the story in which the following text appeared so that the child will understand it in its setting:

"And God created man to His own image: to the image of God He created him: male and female He created them.

And God blessed them, saying: Increase and multiply, and fill the earth, and subdue it, and rule over the fishes of the sea, and the fowls of the air, and all living creatures that move upon the earth" (Gen. i. 26–28).

The children will memorize the text.

10. Adam and Eve leaving Paradise (p. 11).

11. Study pictures in *The Life of the Soul* on Garden of Eden (p. 7) and

12. Read Lesson 1 in *The Life of the Soul* again as a review.

Pupils' Readings:

A Child's Garden of Religion Stories, Chapter 2, "The Garden of Paradise."

Teachers' References:

The Holy Bible.

Teachers' Notes:

IV. Man a Pilgrim

The mottoes and posters for the week may be selected from Lesson 13, *The Life of the Soul* (Man, a Pilgrim on the Road to Heaven).

This lesson will associate itself most naturally with all those that follow. Man is a pilgrim on earth. He is made for God. God in His mercy has given him many helps on the road of life. He has given him the Commandments; He has opened heaven through the Redemption. He has founded the Church to dispense His grace by means of the Sacraments. Particularly He has given us His Son to stay with us in the Holy Eucharist and to become our strengthening food on the road of life. The children should be encouraged to recall these thoughts frequently and to associate them of their own accord with the lessons that follow.

Review:

Why did God create man? Why were Adam and Eve sent out of Paradise? What other punishment did they have to suffer? Could they go to heaven when they died? Why not? Where did they have to go? What did God promise them? When did God keep His promise?

Presentation:

God created man that he may know Him, love Him, and serve Him, and be happy with Him in heaven. When you were born, God gave you to your parents. He wanted them to take care of you and teach you the way to heaven. Parents must help their children to know and love God. If, at the end of your life, you do not get to heaven, God will say to your parents: "Where is that little child I gave you to raise for heaven? Why did you not keep it away from bad companions? Why did you let it do as it pleased, instead of teaching it the way to Me?" And the parents will be punished, if through any fault of theirs, the children are lost. Therefore, children should obey father and mother because the parents must do their duty and bring up their children for God. (See Development 1.)

God made every man for heaven. Life is the road on which man must travel to get there. That is why man is called a Pilgrim. Pilgrim means one who is traveling far away from home. He is a traveler on the road to heaven. He gets tired sometimes, and hungry, and sick. Sometimes he has to suffer much trouble and sorrow before he reaches the end of the way. Death is the end of the way of life. (See Development 2.)

Whether man gets to heaven, will depend upon the road he takes. If you want to go to a large city (name a particular city), will every road take you there? No, some roads will take you farther away. Wouldn't it be foolish, if you were driving, to take the wrong road, and then say: "Oh, well, I'll get there anyway." You would waste a great deal of time and money, and maybe you wouldn't get on the right road in the end. Do you think tourists would do such a foolish thing? And yet, there are people who say, "It does not make any difference what I do or believe. God will take me to heaven in the end even though I do not go the way He wants me to." But God says you cannot go to heaven if you die with a mortal sin on your soul, because then you have left the road which brings you there.

Heaven is a beautiful place. There will be no sorrow there and no death. It will be more beautiful than the Paradise of Adam and Eve, and it will last always and always. (See Development 3.)

Suppose you have committed a mortal sin, what should you do? What happens to people who die with a mortal sin on their souls? Must everybody die? Why? Do children have to die, too? Where do good people go when they die?

Have the pupils read Lesson 13 of *The Life of the Soul* and give them every encouragement for self-expression.

The Text:

Read Lesson 13, *The Life of the Soul* (Man, a Pilgrim on the Road to Heaven).

The text will be used in this lesson as:

1. Introduction to the lesson.
2. Development of the lesson.
3. Summary of the lesson.
4. Review of the lesson.

Content: The particular content of, this lesson will be found by pupils finding out answers to the following questions or answering in the blank spaces the correct words:

What did Adam do after he left Paradise?

.... is the true home of the soul.

Man is a .... on the road to heaven.

How can he keep the road?

What will there be in heaven?

Why is heaven described by the things that are not there?

The Text:

Read Lesson 15, *The Life of the Soul* (The Commandments of God).

The text will be used in this lesson as:

1. Introduction to the lesson.
2. Development of the lesson.
3. Summary of the lesson.
4. Review of the lesson.

Content: The particular content of this lesson will be found by pupils finding out answers to the following questions or answering in the blank spaces the correct words:

Man is a .... on the road to heaven.

Are there any guideposts on the road?

What are they?

Will they help us keep the road?

If we do not keep the commandments, God punishes us in ....

If we do keep the commandments, we will live with God forever in ....

If we are truly sorry for our disobedience to God's commandments what will happen?

Vocabulary: This vocabulary includes the words with religious content or associated with Scriptural narratives.

Lesson 13: pilgrim; everlasting; pure love.

Lesson 15: commandments; hell; forever.

For further development see Developments 4, 5, and 6.

Development:

1. Dramatize "The Prodigal Son," *The American Reader*, III, p. 183, "Finding a Way to Heaven." Find picture of "Prodigal Son" in text (p. 37).

2. Let the pupils make a drawing of *The Pilgrim on the Road to Heaven,* or have them make a sand-table project, showing a

pilgrim going up a road to a steep mountain, to the City of God, other roads leading away from the goal.

3. Discuss with children the necessity of prayer in temptation, and of making an Act of Contrition every evening and after committing sin.

Teach the ejaculation, My Jesus, Mercy, to be used in time of temptation.

4. Poems that may be taught:

"A Brave Man's Hope" — C. Conway

"Oh! Heaven, I Thine Must be Alway" — Father Faber

"Little Things" — Julia A. F. Carney

5. Have the pupils choose one or two good sentences of Lesson 13, *The Life of the Soul* and memorize them.

6. Written language work: Fill the blanks with the following words: tears; heaven; life; God; pilgrim.

a) .... is our true home.

b) Man is a .... on the road of life.

c) Death is the end of the road of ....

d) In heaven we shall see ....

e) In heaven there shall be no more ....

7. Copy these sentences into your religion notebook:

a) In heaven there will be no tears.

b) In heaven there will be no sorrow.

c) In heaven there will be no sickness.

d) In heaven there will be no pain.

e) In heaven there will be no partings.

f) In heaven we shall always be happy.

g) In heaven we shall be with those we love.

h) In heaven we shall see God.

Pupils' Readings:

The Ideal Catholic Reader, III, p. 30, "The Reason Why."

Teachers' References:

To the Heart of a Child, Chap. 16, "Heaven, Hell."

Explanation of the Catechism, Rev. A. Urban; Lesson 1, p. 54, "On the End of Man"; Lesson 5, "On Our First Parents"; Lesson 6, p. 114, "On Sin and Its Kinds."

First Communion, Mother Loyola, Chap. 1, "Eternity and

What the Saints Thought of It"; Chap. 2, "What I Must Think of Eternity."

Teachers' Notes:

V. DOCTRINAL SUMMARY

The Creation

The fundamental facts regarding the Creation, for children of this grade, have been covered. The questions at the end of each lesson have given the child the opportunity to look for the answers which enforce by repetition the principal facts and doctrine regarding the Creation. The form of the answer is guided by the form of the question. The children have now learned the doctrine. By way of summary and review, and giving the student's knowledge definite verbal form, the teacher will have the child learn the formulation of the truths taught in this unit as given in the catechism adopted in the diocese. These truths are:

Baltimore Catechism, No. 2.

Questions 1, 2, 3, 4, 6, 7, 8, 13, 14, 15, 18, 37, 40, 41, 43, 44, 47, 48, 60.[1]

Gasparri's Catechism, for Little Children, I.

Questions 1, 2, 3, 5, 6, 7.

Gasparri's Catechism for Children, II.

Questions 10, 11, 13, 21, 22, 24, 25, 26.

---

[1]These questions and answers are given in the text, *The Life of the Soul.*

UNIT II
THE COMMANDMENTS

Time: From the second week in October to the first week in December, and from the second week in January to the first week in February, inclusive.

I. Keep the Commandments

II. The Ten Commandments

1. The First Commandment
2. The Second Commandment
3. The Third Commandment
4. The Fourth Commandment
5. The Fifth Commandment
6. The Sixth and Ninth Commandments
7. The Seventh and Tenth Commandments
8. The Eighth Commandment
9. The Commandments of the Church

III. Examination of Conscience

Feasts to Remember

October 7, Feast of the Holy Rosary
October 15, St. Teresa
Last Sunday in October, Christ the King
November 1, All Saints
November 2, All Souls
November 21, Presentation

I. Keep the Commandments

For a poster, let the children cut out a guidepost and paste it to one side of the construction paper and then print next to it the words: "Keep the Commandments." The blackboard motto could read: "If thou wilt be perfect, keep the commandments."

Let the children make a "Commandment Booklet," if possible. In it they might write each commandment of God as it is studied week by week and questions that they should ask themselves about each commandment. (For suggestions see *Religion Through Art,* Book III, p. 6.)

Poster or Motto: "If thou wilt enter into life, keep the Commandments."

Pictures:

The Rich Young Man — Hofmann

Review:

Why did God create Adam and Eve? Why did God create you? Could Adam and Eve go to heaven when they died? Why not? Who came to the earth to redeem the world and open heaven again? How long was Jesus the Redeemer, on earth? What did Jesus do when He was thirty years old? Why did He preach to the people?

Presentation:

Suppose you want to make a long trip by car. How will you find the way? What do the guideposts tell you? On our road to heaven God also has put guideposts to point the way. These guideposts are the Ten Commandments. They show the pilgrim who is traveling on the road of life the way to heaven.

Tell the story of the Rich Young Man, emphasizing our Lord's words: "Keep the Commandments." (See Developments 1 and 2.)

We, too, must keep the commandments if we wish to get to heaven, our home.

Would you like to learn these commandments so that you can more easily find the way to heaven? We shall take them one by one and be very attentive so we can learn them well. But first, I am going to tell you the story about the time when God gave the Ten Commandments to man.

II. The Ten Commandments

Pictures:

Giving of the Law on Mount Sinai — Doré

Moses on Mount Sinai, in *The Life of the Soul* (p. 15)

Review:

Where is our true home? What must we do to get to heaven? Will all men go to heaven? Who is in heaven? What did Jesus tell the Rich Young Man when he asked what he must do to get to heaven?

Presentation:

Tell or read the story of Moses Receiving the Ten Commandments. (See Development 3.)

Read Lesson 15, *The Life of the Soul* (review).

For further activities see Developments 4 and 5.

Why did God give us the Ten Commandments? Why does God want us to go to heaven? How can we show our love for Him?

The Text:

Read Lesson 16, *The Life of the Soul* (The Ten Commandments of God).

The text will be used in this lesson as:

    1. Introduction to the lesson.

    2. Development of the lesson.

    3. Summary of the lesson.

    4. Review of the lesson.

Content: The particular content of this lesson will be found by pupils finding the answers to the following questions, or answering in the blank spaces the correct words:

Adam sinned when he .... God's commandment.

I .... when I disobey God's commandments.

God's commandments are binding on all ....

God's commandments are binding on you and on ....

God's commandments are .... in number.

What is the First Commandment of God?

What is the Second Commandment of God?

What is the Third Commandment of God?

What is the Fourth Commandment of God?

What is the Fifth Commandment of God?

What is the Sixth Commandment of God?

What is the Seventh Commandment of God?

What is the Eighth Commandment of God?
What is the Ninth Commandment of God?
What is the Tenth Commandment of God?

The Text:

Read Lesson 17, *The Life of the Soul* (How to Keep the Commandments).

The text will be used in this lesson as:

1. Introduction to the lesson.
2. Development of the lesson.
3. Summary of the lesson.
4. Review of the lesson.

Content: The particular content of this lesson will be found by pupils answering in the blank spaces the correct words:

Who said, "If you would have life keep the Commandments"?

Keep the commandments and you will gain .... life.

Keep the commandments and you will reach your last home with ....

Keep the .... and you will have .... in your soul.

The pure love of God will help you keep the .... of God.

Vocabulary: This vocabulary includes only the words with religious content or associated with Scriptural narratives:

Lesson 16: commandments; Moses; Mount Sinai; binding; Sabbath day; covet; strange; adultery; in vain; false witness.

Lesson 17: life.

Development:

1. Have the children memorize some of the following texts and use them when repeating the story of the Rich Young Man.

"Jesus answered, and said to him. If any one love Me, he will keep My word, and My Father will love him, and We will come to him, and will make Our abode with him" (John xiv. 23).

"Master, which is the great commandment in the Law? Jesus said to him: Thou shalt love the Lord, thy God, with thy whole heart, and with thy whole soul, and with thy whole mind. This is the greatest and the first commandment. And the second is like to this: Thou shalt love thy neighbor as thyself. On these two commandments dependeth the whole law and the prophets" (Matt. xxii. 36–40).

"If thou wilt enter into life, keep the commandments" (Matt. xix. 13).

2. Let a child impersonate the Rich Young Man, and tell the class about his visit to Jesus and what Jesus said to him. Have children use Scripture texts in the narrative.

3. Read "The Ten Commandments" — *A Child's Garden,* Chap. 15.

4. Pupils make a clay tile and trace on it the Tablets of the Commandments, or let them draw the two Tablets in their notebooks and write the words: "If I want to go to heaven, I must keep the commandments."

5. Discuss the picture *The Fourth Commandment,* by Sinkel.

Pupils' Readings:

A Child's Garden of Religion Stories, Chapter 15, "The Ten Commandments."

Columbus, III, pp. 80–85, "Miriam's Wish," "Moses in the Bulrushes."

Ideal, pp. 203–205, "Moses."

Teachers' References:

The Faith for Little Children, M. Eaton, pp. 41–88, "The Commandments."

The Spiritual Way, M. Eaton, pp. 70–80; 93–106, "The Spiritual Way."

The Story Ever New, M. Eaton, p. 121.

First Course in Religion, MacEachen, pp. 110–114.

Explanation of the Catechism, Spirago, pp. 284–286, "The Two Commandments of Charity."

Charity Toward the Neighbor, Spirago, pp. 295–297.

The Ten Commandments, Spirago, pp. 306–309.

Sunday School Teacher's Explanation of the Catechism, Rev. A. Urban, p. 326.

Teachers' Notes:

1. The First Commandment

"I am the Lord, thy God. Thou shalt not have strange
gods before Me."

Have posters made with mission pictures; also with pictures
of children at prayer. The words, "In prayer we talk to God,"
may be used as a motto.

Pictures:

The Christ Child — Ittenbach

Mary, the Mother of God

Saints, Idols — (Cut from mission magazines)

See Development 1.

Review:

To whom did God give the commandments? Why did God
give us the Ten Commandments? Why does He want us to go
to heaven? How can we show our love for Him? What leads us
away from the right road to heaven? How can we get back on
the right road? What helps did God give us to keep us on the
right road?

Presentation:

Explain simply the meaning of the First Commandment;
mentioning particularly those faults of which young children are
usually guilty.

There is only one true God. Our parents, the priest, and the
teachers in the Catholic school help us to know about the one
true God. Therefore, when they speak to us about Him, we
should listen attentively. God is good and loves us very much.
Nothing makes Him angry with us except sin. In the First Commandment God tells us that we must adore Him alone. We honor
God especially by praying with devotion. The Blessed Virgin and
the saints are the friends of God. Therefore we also honor them
and ask them to pray for us. We should try to love God and
make sacrifices as the saints did. Above all, we should honor
God's dear Mother and show a special love for her. She is our
mother in heaven and she loves us because God loves us. (See
Developments 2 and 3.)

There are many people who do not know about the one true God. We must pray for them, because God made them as well as us, and He is their Father as well as ours. (See Developments 4 and 5.)

Ask yourself: Did I say my morning and evening prayers every day? Did I think of God while I was talking or praying to Him?

Read for review, Lesson 10 in *The Life of the Soul.*

Further activities are suggested in Developments 6 to 10.

Development:

1. Teach a hymn in honor of the Blessed Virgin. One of the following will be appropriate:

> Mother Mary, at Thine Altar
> Mother, at Your Feet is Kneeling

2. Remind the children to say morning and evening prayers each day and to remember that in prayer they talk to God.

3. Review and explain the Acts of Faith, Hope, and Charity.

4. Speak of the missionaries who go to pagan lands to teach the people about God. Discuss with the class what can be done by children to help convert the pagans. Interest them in missionary magazines and in mission activities, such as collecting stamps, buying heathen babies, etc. Try to make the interest a lasting one so that they will desire to continue the work as they grow older. (See *Practical Aids,* p. 232.)

5. In the mission magazines are frequently found pictures of Jesus surrounded by children of different races. Have the pupils find such pictures and write a few sentences about them.

6. Speak of the Feast of All Saints and in preparation for the the feast have each child find out who is his patron saint.

7. Have the pupils find stories of the saints in different books and relate them to the class.

8. Show pictures of children at prayer and have the class discuss them.

9. Continue the "Commandment Booklet."

10. Poems to study or read:

"Your Friends" — M. D. Thayer

"In the Morning" — M. D. Thayer

"Morning Prayer" — Robert H. Benson

"Saying Grace" — R. L. Stevenson

Pupils' Readings:

A Child's Garden of Religion Stories, p. 128, "The Golden Calf."

American Reader, II, p. 41, "A Child's Prayer."

Ideal Catholic, III, p. 55, "Day and Night"; p. 11, "God Heard Fred's Prayer."

De la Salle, III, p. 134, "Prayer Before Meals."

Religion Course, II, MacEachen, pp. 30–34, "The First Commandment."

Teachers' References:

Teaching the Ten Commandments, S. M. Agnesine, pp. 7–54, "The First and Second Commandments."

Catholic Educational Series, Religion Book, III, pp. 13–21, "Faith, Hope, Charity."

Practical Aids, p. 36, "Faith"; p. 80, "Prayers Before and After Meals"; p. 114, "Despair of Judas."

The Catechism Explained, Spirago, pp. 309–338, "First Commandment."

Teacher Tells a Story, Vol. II, pp. 25–49, "Faith"; pp. 193–205, "Prayer"; pp. 69–78, "The Name of Jesus."

Sunday School Teacher's Explanation of the Catechism, Rev A. Urban, Lessons 30–31, "On the First Commandment, On the Honor and Invocation of the Saints."

Teachers' Notes:

2. The Second Commandment

"Thou shalt not take the name of the Lord thy God in vain."

Mottoes for blackboard or posters:

Blessed be God
Blessed be the name of Jesus
Hallowed be Thy name
See Developments 1, 2, and 3.

Pictures:

Samuel — Reynolds

Review:

Why did God give us the commandments? To whom did He give them? What is the First Commandment? How should we say our prayers? When should we pray? Does God hear us pray? Why?

Review what has been said about the First Commandment including the faults committed against this commandment.

Presentation:

Explain the Second Commandment. God is our Father. We love God because He made us and gave us all we have. He loved us so much that He died for us. When we love people very much we honor them. We do not use their names in an angry or disrespectful way. The Second Commandment tells us that we must not use the name of God in vain, but must respect and honor it. We say every day: "Hallowed be Thy name." By that prayer we ask God that we may know and love Him more every day. If we do that, we will always use His name with great love and respect. When we hear the name of Jesus, our best Friend, we should bow our head. We should never be ashamed to let everyone know that we honor Him. We may never curse or use God's name in an improper way. When we hear people using the name of God in vain we should go away from them. We should also say a little prayer like "Hallowed be Thy name" or "Praised be Jesus Christ" to make up for the disrespect to God. We may not speak disrespectfully of the saints or of holy things.

Remind the children of their First Holy Communion and encourage them to keep that tongue, which will soon receive the good Jesus, from uttering His name with disrespect.

Ask yourself: Did I use the Holy Name in anger? Did I use the name of God or of holy things disrespectfully? Did I think of God while I was talking or praying to Him?

Read Lesson 11 in *The Life of the Soul*. Make use of this and succeeding lessons that serve as a review to impress upon the children the fact that God punishes those who disobey His commands.

For other activities see Developments 4, 5, and 6.

Development:

1. Teach the children to bow their heads at the name of Jesus.

2. Teach short ejaculations for the children to say whenever they hear the name of God or of holy things used in vain. The following are recommended: "Jesus," "Mary," "Blessed be God," "Blessed be the name of Jesus."

3. In this connection explain the meaning of "Hallowed be Thy name."

4. Speak of the respect due to priests and sisters: Discuss with the class, different ways in which this respect can be shown.

5. The following poems may be studied or read:

"Different Ways" — M. D. Thayer (*The Life of the Soul*, p. 41).

"Your Friends" — M. D. Thayer

"The Name of Mary" — Adelaide Procter

"Growing" — M. D. Thayer

6. Have the pupils find stories about martyrs who refused to show irreverence to God and holy things.

7. Continue the "Commandment Booklet."

Pupils' Readings:

American Cardinal, III, p. 177, "St. Dorothy, God Given."

Ideal, III, p. 62, "The Shepherd Boy."

Wonder Stories of God's People, p. 313, "St. Ignatius of Antioch."

American Cardinal, III, p. 186, "San Min's Treasure."

Catholic Educational Series, Third Reader, p. 191, "The Little Martyr of the Blessed Sacrament."

Religion Course, II, MacEachen, "The Second Commandment."

Teachers' References:

Catechist's Manual, Religion, Second Course, MacEachen, "Second Commandment."

The Catechism Explained, Spirago, pp. 339–346, "Second Commandment."

Sunday School Teacher's Explanation of the Catechism, Rev. A. Urban, pp. 343–354, "On the Second Commandment."

Teaching the Ten Commandments, S. M. Agnesine, "The Second Commandment."

Teacher Tells a Story, Vol. 11, pp. 69–78, "The Name of Jesus."

Teachers' Notes:

3. The Third Commandment

"Remember thou keep holy the Sabbath Day."

Motto or poster: "God rested on the seventh day."

Encourage the children to make other posters with appropriate slogans and pictures.

Pictures:

Pilgrims Going to Church — Boughton

The Last Supper — Da Vinci

Review:

Why did God give us the commandments? What is the First Commandment? The Second? What does God command by the Second Commandment? What did God do on the seventh day of creating?

Presentation:

Explain the Third Commandment. (See Developments 1 and 2.)

God wants people to work, but He does not want them to work so hard that they have no time to think of Him. God made us all for heaven. But some people are so busy working for themselves that they forget all about heaven. Therefore God said in the Third Commandment, "Remember thou keep holy the Sabbath day." Sabbath means rest. God says that we should not work on the Sabbath day. God made us for Himself. He gave us so many things we should think of Him often and thank Him for all His gifts. We should try to give Him as much time on Sunday as we can. We keep the Sabbath holy by hearing Mass. It is not enough just to go to church. We must be careful to come in time and we must say our prayers and listen to the sermon. (See Developments 3 and 4.)

Ask yourself: Did I miss Mass on Sundays through my own fault? Did I come too late to hear an entire Mass? Did I talk and misbehave in church?

Read in *The Life of the Soul,* Lesson 12, and point out in this connection that the soul of man is strengthened and nourished by prayer. Many people do not take much time for prayer during the week. God, therefore, set aside Sunday so that people might have more time to think of Him and their souls.

See Developments 5, 6, and 7 for other activities.

The Text:

Read Lesson 18, *The Life of the Soul* (The Pure Love of God).

The text will be used in this lesson as:

1. Introduction to the lesson.
2. Development of the lesson.
3. Summary of the lesson.
4. Review of the lesson.

Content: The particular content of this lesson will be found by pupils finding out answers to the following questions or answering in the blank spaces the correct words:

If I am loyal to God..........

1. I shall show my .... in God.
2. I shall show my .... of God.
3. I shall say little .... to God, in the morning and at night.
4. I shall say little .... to God whenever I have a bad thought or want to do something that is not right.

What questions can I ask myself to help me keep the First Commandment of God?

What questions can I ask myself to help me keep the Second Commandment of God?

What questions can I ask myself to help me keep the Third Commandment of God?

What three commandments teach us to love God?

What is the First Commandment of God?

What is the Second Commandment of God?

What is the Third Commandment of God?

Vocabulary: This vocabulary includes the words with religious content or associated with Scriptural narratives:

Religion; angry; trust; love; necessary; reverently; dreams; faith; holyday of obligation.

Development:

1. Have the children bring as many pictures as they can, showing people at prayer in church, reverence in church, etc. Give them a chance for free discussion of the pictures and their meaning.

2. Insist that the children use their prayer books during Mass. A study of this commandment will make them see more clearly the necessity of prayer and good behavior in church.

3. Give a simple explanation or review of the essential parts of the Mass; also a general idea of the Canon of the Mass.

4. Let them paste in their "Commandment Booklet" a picture referring to the Mass and write a sentence about it.

5. Review the various acts of reverence used in church, such as genuflecting, bowing the head, using holy water. Boys should show reverence when passing a church by tipping the hat, and girls by bowing the head.

Let them bring to class any pictures illustrating the sacredness of Sunday.

6. Teach the following quotations:

"Thine is the day, and Thine is the night" (Ps. 73. 16).

"The Lord blessed the seventh day and sanctified it" (Exod. xx. 11).

"Remember that thou keep holy the Sabbath Day."

7. One of the following poems may be taught:
"Two Went Into the Temple to Pray" — Richard Crashaw
"God's Home" — E. F. Garesché
"Please" — M. D. Thayer

Pupils' Readings:
Catholic Educational Series Religion Third Reader, pp. 175–181, "The Last Supper"; p. 190, "A Child's Wish."

Teachers' References:
The Catechism Explained, Spirago, pp. 246–357, "Third Commandment."

Teaching the Ten Commandments, pp. 55–71.

Sunday School Teacher's Explanation of the Catechism, Rev. A. Urban, pp. 354–359.

Teacher Tells a Story, Vols. I and II.

Tell Us Another, Herbst

Text Books of Religion Third Grade, pp. 57–59.

Teachers' Notes:

4. The Fourth Commandment

"Honor thy father and thy mother."

Have the children choose short mottoes of their own, from poems or stories for blackboard or poster use. As this commandment is so important, the mottoes may be changed from day to day and a variety of posters added. (See Development 1.)

Pictures:
The Fourth Commandment — Sinkel

Other pictures of obedient, helpful children, should be used.

Review:
Name two commandments you have learned so far. What does each commandment tell us to do or not to do? Why should we keep the Sunday holy? How can we keep the Sunday holy?

Why should we show reverence in church? By what sign can you tell that you are in a Catholic Church where God is present on the altar?

Presentation:

The Holy Bible, which is the work of God, tells us that Jesus was subject to His parents from the time He was a little boy until He left His house at the age of thirty. "He was subject to them" means that He obeyed them in all things. Jesus was God and did not have to obey anyone. But He wanted to teach us what we must do to get to heaven. Therefore, He Himself showed us how we must act toward our parents and those who have charge of us. We should honor our parents, love them, obey them, and pray for them. God promised those who keep the Fourth Commandment a special blessing. (See Developments 2 and 3.)

Our teachers take the place of our parents. We must obey our teachers in school just as we should obey our parents at home. We must also obey the laws of our country and respect the officers who carry out the law. (See Developments 5 and 6.)

It is wrong to disobey our parents and teachers. God is displeased with children who talk back to their parents and who are stubborn and disobedient. No one likes a bad and stubborn and disobedient child. Everyone loves an obedient child. Parents love their children and try to do all for their good. Children do not always understand or know what is good for them, but when they grow up they will see their parents were right. (See Developments 7, 8, and 9.)

Ask yourself: Did I disobey my parents? Was I stubborn and mean toward my parents? Did I disobey my teachers? Did I make fun of old people?

Review the story of Adam and Eve in *The Life of the Soul* and stress their disobedience to God. Point out at the same time that parents take the place of God.

Continue the study of *The Life of the Soul,* Lesson 19.

Development:

1. Use the Scripture texts whenever possible during this week. Let the children write them in their "Commandment Booklet."

"Honor thy father and thy mother."

"And He was subject to them" (Luke ii. 51).

2. Let the children tell of the many little ways in which Jesus showed His love and obedience at home. Use as many pictures as possible to help their imagination along.

3. Have the pupils give practical examples of honor, love, and help of parents.

4. Require some of the children to find little stories, poems, and quotations pertaining to obedience and post these in a conspicuous place or have them read or recited to the class.

5. Dramatize some little story or poem that brings out obedience to authority. "Which Loved Mother Best," *Ideal Third Reader*, p. 25, would serve as a good guessing game when dramatized by a group of children. Class discussion should follow.

Have the children make copious use of the many problems and suggestions given in *Teaching the Ten Commandments*, pp. 72–92.

6. Take this opportunity to inculcate safety rules from the viewpoint of obedience to authority.

7. Remind the children of their obligation to pray daily for their parents. Have them find a little prayer for their parents in their prayer books; or better still, have them make their own simple prayer such as: "Dear Jesus, bless my parents and help me always to be good to them." Plan with them a certain convenient time each day at which to say the prayer, either at Mass, after Holy Communion, or at their evening prayer, so as to help them establish the habit.

8. Encourage children to do a kind act for mother and father, every day. Also encourage the children to tell mother and father everything, good and bad, that they have done during the day.

Make a picture booklet of "Kind Deeds," covering these points:

1. Kindness to fathers and mothers.
   a) Show affection.
   b) Help in small ways.
   c) Be courteous.

2. Kindness to schoolmates and classmates.

   a) A willing helpfulness.

   b) Not to talk and disturb others at school.

   c) To show regard for the rights of others in games.

   d) To be careful of all school property.

3. Kindness to my neighbors means:

   a) To be careful of their lawns and shrubbery.

   b) Not to annoy them by noisy playing when they are resting.

   c) To be kind to their pets (Cf. Coleridge's "He prayeth Best").

9. Have the pupils study one of the poems suggested in Pupils' Readings.

Pupils' Readings:

Ideal, III, p. 25, "Which Loved Mother Best"; p. 21, "A Grain of Sand"; p. 85, "Only One"; p. 86. "Helping Mother"; p. 179, "Obedience."

Rosary, III, p. 103, "Hush-Bye"; p. 88, "Elizabeth"; p. 20, "David Winks."

Continue the "Commandment Booklet."

Teachers' References:

Practical Aids, pp. 39–44, "Obedience."

The Catechism Explained, Spirago, pp. 371–380, "The Fourth Commandment."

Sunday School Teacher's Explanation of the Catechism, Rev. A. Urban, pp. 359–367, "The Fourth Commandment."

Teaching the Ten Commandments, pp. 72–92.

Ideal Third Reader, p. 25.

Teachers' Notes:

5. The Fifth Commandment

"Thou shalt not kill."

Many posters and mottoes on kindness, health, and safety suggest themselves for this week's lesson.

The entire work of the week may easily be developed into a "kindness project" or a "health project." (See Development 1.)

Continue the study of *The Life of the Soul*, Lesson 19 (Love of Neighbor).

Pictures:

The Murder of Abel — Doré

Pictures illustrating kindness.

Review:

Review the commandments already taught, especially the fourth. Why should we love and obey our parents? What should we do to show our love for our parents? What did God promise to those who obey their parents? What is the great commandment Jesus told the Rich Young Man about?

Presentation:

We are all God's children. He created us, and He loves us. He also wants us to love others for His sake. In the Fifth Commandment God forbids us to harm ourselves or others. Our bodies belong to Him because He created them. We can harm ourselves or others in body and in soul. We harm our bodies by eating or drinking too much or by exposing ourselves to danger without cause. Children should obey the rules of health and safety for the sake of protecting their bodies as God wants. (See Developments 2 and 3.)

Our Lord also tells us that we must not get angry. We must try to put angry thoughts out of our minds. In the "Our Father" we pray "Forgive us our trespasses." By those words we mean to say, "Please, Lord, forgive us, as we forgive them who try to harm us." We should not make others angry. Our Lord says: "Do unto others as you would have others do unto you." (See Developments 4 and 5.)

It is bad to kill the body, but it is worse to kill the soul. Mortal sin kills the soul. When we make others commit a mortal sin we kill the soul. Sometimes children make others commit sin by giving them a bad example. Always be careful not to give bad example and not to make others commit sin. (See Development 6.)

Ask yourself: Was I angry? Stubborn? Did I fight with others? Was I jealous? Did I try to "Get even" with others? Did I make others commit sin? What sin? Did I lead others into sin by my bad example? Was I unkind or mean to others? Was I cruel to animals?

During this and succeeding lessons until two weeks before Christmas read and study Lesson 19 in *The Life of the Soul* and if necessary review some of the earlier reading lessons.

For further activities see Developments 7, 8, and 9.

Development:

1. Teach or review rules of health and safety that the children ought to know and frequently refer to the fact that our bodies must be kept clean and healthy because they belong to God.

2. Have the children dramatize or pantomime little acts to bring out the thought that we should do unto others as we would have done to ourselves. For example, it is time for school. A little boy who is in a hurry drops his books and pencil box. Some children hurry by but do not help him. One stops and helps him pick up his books and pencils.

3. Let the children dramatize the Good Samaritan or other pertinent stories.

4. For oral language work let the children tell of little acts of kindness they have seen others do.

5. Write during the language period a short story about a kind deed you have seen or heard about.

6. Teach self-control in little things. Let the children give practical examples from school and home. Discuss with them the necessity of self-control and the evils of a lack of self-control.

7. Encourage the children to play with the child who seems to be neglected by others.

8. Teach kindness to animals.

9. Have the pupils look up Bible History and other stories to

illustrate phases of the Fifth Commandment, as "The Good Samaritan," "The Crucifixion," the kindness of Jesus to the poor and sick.

10. Continue the "Commandment Booklet."

Pupils' Readings:

American Catholic, III, p. 44, "The Lily and the Rose"; p. 57, "Prince Harweda."

Columbus, III, p. 197, "Damon and Pythias."

Corona, III, p. 169, "Nobility."

Ideal Catholic, III, p. 99, "Ethel King"; "The Frog's Cousin."

Religion Course, II, MacEachen, p. 40, "Fifth Commandment."

Standard Catholic, III, p. 55, "Androclus and the Lion"; p. 179, "A Lesson of Mercy."

Wonder Stories, p. 338, "St. Philip's Lesson."

Teachers' References:

Practical Aids, "Kindness, Patience, Gentleness."

The Catechism Explained, Spirago, pp. 380–391, "The Fifth Commandment."

Sunday School Teacher's Explanation of the Catechism, Rev. A. Urban, pp. 367–373, "The Fifth Commandment."

Teaching the Ten Commandments, pp. 93–104, "Fifth Commandment."

Teachers' Notes:

6. Sixth and Ninth Commandments

"Thou shalt not commit adultery."

"Thou shalt not covet thy neighbor's wife."

There are many beautiful selections from which the pupils may choose their posters or mottoes for this week.

God sees me
Think about beautiful things
Look only at beautiful things
"Beautiful faces are those that show
Beautiful thoughts that lie below"
Blessed are the clean of heart

This week let pupils learn or review a hymn or poem to the Blessed Virgin or the Guardian Angel in connection with this lesson, such as:

> Mother Dear, Oh, Pray for Me
> Dear Angel, Ever at My Side
> The Child to the Guardian Angel

Write a few suitable Scripture texts on the board and quote them as occasion presents itself in the course of the week:

"He that loveth cleanness of heart shall have the King for his friend" (Prov. xxii. 11).

"Blessed are the clean of heart, for they shall see God" (Matt. v. 3–10).

"The impure shall not possess the kingdom of heaven" (I Cor. vi. 9.)

"Be holy, because I, the Lord your God, am holy" (Lev. xix. 2).

Continue the study of *The Life of the Soul*, Lesson 19 (Love of Neighbor).

Pictures:

The Immaculate Conception — Murillo
The Age of Innocence — Reynolds
Pictures of saints bearing lilies.

Review:

What is the Fifth Commandment? What does God teach us in the Fifth Commandment? Why must we be careful not to harm ourselves or others? Tell some ways in which we can keep our bodies from harm. Which is worse to kill the body or the soul? How can we kill the soul? How can mortal sin be taken away from the soul?

Presentation:

We know that God sees and knows everything we say or do

or think. We should, therefore, never do or think anything of which we would be ashamed before God. We must be clean in our thoughts, words, and looks. A child of God is always careful to use his eyes, hands, and all other parts of the body as God intended they should be used. God made our bodies. When Jesus comes to us in Holy Communion we are like the tabernacle in the church, because Jesus is in our hearts. Just think how good and pure we ought to keep ourselves so that Jesus will love to come to us often. In order to keep good and pure, we should pray to God, to our Blessed Mother, and to our Guardian Angel to help us. But we must also keep away from bad companions, from boys and girls who talk about bad things, or do bad things, and try to instill into the children's hearts a great love of all that is pure and beautiful. (See Developments 1 and 2.) Dwell particularly on the beauty of innocence and purity. Show by examples how God loves the pure of heart. He chose Mary as His Mother, St. Joseph as His foster father. (See Development 3.)

If the children are to receive their First Holy Communion during this year, encourage them to direct their thoughts to prepare their hearts for His coming, day by day, by trying to keep themselves as free from sin as possible and by thinking only beautiful thoughts, reading beautiful things, looking only at beautiful things, listening to beautiful things. Remind them often of the coming of Jesus and when occasion presents itself and you have created a longing for Him in their souls, pause a moment and let them say softly and reverently:

> "Jesus, Jesus come to me,
> Oh, how much I long for Thee."

(See Development 4.)

Make clear to the children the difference between temptation and sin, also the difference between what is only vulgar and what is actually sinful. Point out the necessity of keeping the body clean as well as the soul. (See Development 5.)

Ask yourself: Did I talk about impure things? Did I listen to impure talk? Did I want impure thoughts? Did I teach others to commit impure sins?

Development:

1. Have the children make a lily poster. Let them write their favorite sayings in their "Commandment Booklets."

2. Teach the ejaculation: "O Mary conceived without sin, pray for us who have recourse to thee."

3. Have the class find stories about saints who loved purity above all else.

4. Encourage the pupils to make special visits to church to tell Jesus how much they want to receive Him into their hearts.

5. Discuss with the class some little quotation like the following:

"The eyes are the windows of the soul."

"It is better to be alone than in bad company."

"Birds of a feather flock together."

"Beautiful faces are those that show
Beautiful thoughts that lie below."

Pupils' Readings:

Heroes of God's Church, Matimore.

A Child's Garden, p. 222, "Jesus and the Little Children."

Catholic Educational Series, III, p. 174, "St. Agnes."

Text Book of Religion, III, Yorke, p. 63.

The Story of the Little Flower.

Teachers' References:

The Catechism Explained, Spirago, "The Sixth Commandment."

Sunday School Teacher's Explanation of the Catechism, Rev. A. Urban, "The Sixth Commandment."

Practical Aids.

Teachers' Notes:

7. Seventh and Tenth Commandments

"Thou shalt not steal."

"Thou shalt not covet thy neighbor's goods."

The following are suggested for posters and mottoes:

Thou shalt not steal

Dare to do right

God sees me

God knows all things

Pictures:

The Temptation of Christ — Scheffer

Review:

Which commandment tells us to keep the Sunday holy? To say our prayers with devotion? Not to use the name of God in vain? To obey our parents? To be pure in thought, word, and deed? (See Development 1.)

Presentation:

In the Seventh Commandment God tells us not to take or keep what does not belong to us. No matter how small the thing is, we should not take it if it is not ours. Children who begin by taking little things, never stop there but by and by take bigger things, until at last they become wicked thieves. We ought not take anything even from our own homes without first asking. Our Lord said: "He that is unjust in that which is little, is unjust also in that which is greater." (See Development 2.)

We must not think that no one will know when we steal. God knows, because He sees everything we do. If we take something that does not belong to us, we must give it back if possible. If we borrow anything, we must return it. To borrow and not to return is the same as stealing. (See Development 3.)

God also wants us to take care not to damage other people's property, such as fences and windows. In school and in church the furniture and other things are for our use, but they do not belong to us. Therefore, we may not injure books or furniture in school or church. We should also be careful of our own books and clothes and not spoil or injure them willfully.

The Tenth Commandment tells us we must not want to get

by unjust means the things that other people have. God gives us everything we need. We must drive away all greedy and unhappy thoughts and not wish for things we cannot have. Children who are always wanting a great many things they cannot have, soon learn to take what does not belong to them. We should thank God for what we have and be satisfied. Jesus Himself was very poor and always loved the poor people. (See Developments 4 and 5.)

Ask yourself: Did I steal or help others steal? Did I take from home without permission what did not belong to me? Did I keep what I found? Did I damage other people's property?

For further suggestions see Developments 6 and 9.

Development:

1. Have the children tell the story of the "Temptation of Christ" and show the picture.

2. Encourage the children to find stories in different readers, of people whose honesty was rewarded.

3. Instruct children that stolen goods must be restored before absolution can be received, that damaged goods must be paid for, and that hired people must do honest work.

4. There are many beautiful pictures of Christ in the homes of the poor, among others *Christ in the House of Peasants,* by L'Hermite. If you can get some of these pictures, use them for an oral or written lesson, and try to impress upon the children Christ's love for the poor.

5. Have children show from the life of Jesus that He was poor.

Suggest to the children to look up the *Life of St. Francis of Assisi* and discuss it in class. Let a bright student who gets his lessons quickly, read and tell the class the story of Judas, pointing out how his greed for money caused him to sell Jesus for thirty pieces of silver.

6. Let pupils find and recite to the class, or post on the bulletin board, little sayings and poems about honesty. For example: "An honest man is the noblest work of God." — *Pope.*

7. Give the children concrete problems to establish correct principles of conduct; for example: Jack Lane threw a ball to

his friend. It went through a neighbor's window. What should Jack do?

a) Run away and not tell because he can't pay for it?

b) Say that another boy threw the ball?

c) Go to the neighbor and ask what he should do about it?

8. Encourage children to read and repeat Bible History stories of the New Testament which have some bearing on this commandment: Birth of Christ in Poverty; Rich Young Man; The Rich Man and Lazarus; Despair of Judas. Let them tell other stories they know on this commandment.

9. Use suggested problems on the grade level of the class in *Teaching the Ten Commandments*, pp. 149–160.

10. Continue the "Commandment Booklet."

Pupils' Readings:

American Catholic, III, p. 50, "The Jeweled Pencil."

Rosary, III, p. 28, "David Makes a Mistake"; p. 42, "David Makes Another Mistake."

Teachers' References:

The Catechism Explained, Spirago, pp. 149–170, "Seventh and Tenth Commandments."

Sunday School Teacher's Explanation of the Catechism, Rev. A. Urban, pp. 359–381, "Seventh and Tenth Commandments."

Practical Aids, pp. 54–57, "Truthfulness."

Teaching the Ten Commandments, pp. 149–170.

Teachers' Notes:

8. The Eighth Commandment

"Thou shalt not bear false witness against thy neighbor."

For posters or mottoes use the following or similar quotations:

"Do unto others as you would have them to do unto you."

"Speak the truth and bear the blame."

"Stand by your conscience, your honor, your faith,
Stand like a hero and battle to death." — *Wilson.*

Have the pupils find mottoes, and short sayings of their own. (See Development 1.)

Continue the Study of *The Life of the Soul,* Lesson 19 (Love of Neighbor).

Review:

What is the Seventh Commandment? The Tenth? What are we forbidden by the Seventh and Tenth Commandments? Why should we be careful not to take even the smallest things that do not belong to us? Ought we to take things from home without asking? What must people do who have stolen something? What must those do who have damaged other people's property? May you keep what you find?

Presentation:

God tells us in the Eighth Commandment that we may not tell a lie. We must always speak and act the truth. God loves the truth and hates a lie. A lie is mean and cowardly. If we don't want to be mean cowards, we must speak the truth no matter how hard it is. If we tell a lie, we soon have to tell more and more lies to cover up the first one. In that way we fall deeper and deeper into sin. We shall always be afraid of being found out and become unhappy. No one wants to believe a child who is always lying, but everyone loves an honest, sincere child. (See Development 2.)

God also forbids us in this commandment to say anything about others that is not true or to talk about their faults except to those who have a right to know. We do not like it when others talk about us, especially when what they say is not true, and we must be just as careful to treat others as we should like to be treated ourselves. (See Developments 3 and 4.)

Ask yourself: Did I tell a lie? Did I act a lie? Do I talk about the faults of others? Do I say things about others that are not true? Do I pretend to be better than I really am?

See Developments 5, 6, and 7.

The Text:

Read Lesson 19, *The Life of the Soul* (Love of Neighbor).
The text will be used in this lesson as:

1. Introduction to the lesson.
2. Development of the lesson.
3. Summary of the lesson.
4. Review of the lesson.

Content: The particular content of this lesson will be found
by pupils finding out answers to the following questions:

What commandment teaches us the love of neighbor?

Name three good reasons why we should love our neighbor

What is the Fourth Commandment of God?

What is the Fifth Commandment of God?

What is the Sixth Commandment of God?

What is the Seventh Commandment of God?

What is the Eighth Commandment of God?

What is the Ninth Commandment of God?

What is the Tenth Commandment of God?

What questions kept in mind will help the soul honor father
and mother?

What questions kept in mind will help the soul to respect the
life of the neighbor?

What questions kept in mind will help the soul act modestly
toward our neighbor?

What questions kept in mind will help the soul act honestly
toward the property of our neighbor?

Vocabulary: This vocabulary includes the words with religious
content or associated with Scriptural narratives:

Immodest; steal.

Development:

1. Have children find poems and quotations that speak of
truthfulness. The best poem may be chosen by the class for
study.

2. Divide the class into groups and have them dramatize
simple stories bringing out truthfulness.

3. Encourage the children never to speak of the faults of
others but to tell only the good things they do. Give them a

chance to carry out this suggestion by letting them tell the class some good acts done by a boy or girl they know, by the neighbor, etc.

4. Suggest to the children that they form a resolution that when they are tempted to tell a lie to say, "Jesus help me!" and then bravely speak the truth.

5. Tell the class a story showing that it takes a great deal of courage sometimes to tell the truth.

6. Have the pupils suggest actual life situations pertaining to truthfulness and discuss them with the class. For example, Mary comes home late from school because she was punished. Her mother asks her where she was.

7. Things for the children to find out: Who told the first lie? Who told a lie to the Three Kings? Who acted a lie at the Last Supper? What Apostle told a lie and was sorry for it all his life? What great statesman of our country is noted for his truthfulness as a boy?

8. Continue the "Commandment Booklet."

Pupils' Readings:

Religion Second Course, MacEachen, "The Eighth Commandment."

A Child's Garden of Religion Stories, "The Ten Commandments."

Teachers' References:

The Catechism Explained, Spirago, pp. 400–412, "The Eighth Commandment."

Sunday School Teacher's Explanation of the Catechism, Rev. A. Urban, pp. 388–395, "The Eighth Commandment."

Practical Aids, pp. 58–59, "Honesty."

Teacher Tells a Story.

Teaching the Ten Commandments.

Teachers' Notes:

9. The Commandments of the Church

Review:

The Act of Contrition should be reviewed at this time and the meaning of the words carefully explained.

Presentation:

For children of this grade the commandments to hear Mass on Sundays and holydays, to abstain from meat on Fridays, to make the Easter Duties, to help to the support of the Church by their Sunday offerings, are of practical value. Discussion of problems suggested by the children will make a few profitable and interesting class periods. The "Commandment Booklet" could include the Commandments of the Church. (See Developments 1 to 4.)

As the Holydays of Obligation occur, recall what has been studied about them.

Development:

1. Have the children study the Commandments of the Church.

2. Teach the Holydays of Obligation and have the children finish the booklet by writing carefully the Holydays of Obligation.

3. If there are windows, paintings, or other representation of some particular feasts, call the children's attention to them and have them discuss their meaning.

4. It may be well to impress upon the class in a simple way the right of the Church to make laws. The subject of Church authority will be more fully studied later in the year, however.

III. Examination of Conscience

Motto: "If at first you do not succeed, try, try again."

Pictures:

The Consoling Christ — Plockhorst

Infant Samuel — Reynolds

Children Praying at Mother's Knee

Review:

Spend a full period reviewing the Ten Commandments.

Presentation:

When we learned about the Ten Commandments, we heard what God wants us to do or not to do. When you asked yourselves the questions, a voice inside of you said: "You did that; you told a lie often"; or "You quarreled, you were jealous." What is that little voice inside of you called? It is called *conscience*. It is really the voice of God in your heart. You should try always to listen to that voice. In that way you will remain a child of God. (See Development 2.)

I know a little girl who, every night before she goes to bed, tells her mother everything naughty that she did during the day. Then she kneels down at her mother's side and tells God how sorry she is. Every child should think over his sins before going to bed and then tell God how sorry he is. (See Development 3.)

Ask yourself: What wrong did I do today in church? In school? At home? In the street? Alone? With others?

Development:

1. Teach one of the following poems, and read as many others as possible:

"God Sees" — Mary Mapes Dodge

"Content and Rich" — Rev. Robt. Southwell, S.J.

"Speak, Little Voice" — Rev. M. Earls, S.J.

See *Practical Aids,* p. 137, for other poems.

2. Show exactly how a child should examine his conscience every evening. The process should be as simple as possible and should be followed by an Act of Contrition. Children should be taught to examine their conscience every night. They should be reminded before leaving school in the evening and asked in the morning whether they have remembered. Care must be taken to make the act desirable rather than disagreeable. A habit well established at this time is generally carried through life.

3. Tell the children that if they are really sorry for their sins, God, their good Father, will forgive them, at once, if they promise to go to confession. Then they will feel good and happy when they go to bed, their Guardian Angel will be happy too. The Blessed Virgin will love them again, no matter how naughty they were during the day. Then, if their soul is clean

and they love God with all their heart, they will not need to be afraid day or night, for nobody can harm them. Teach them that if they have been naughty to father or mother, to go to them and ask their pardon.

4. Copy the following selections in the "Commandment Booklet":

> Little children, love each other;
> Show true love to great and small
> Love your father and your mother,
> And love God most of all.

5. Make a little folder, paste a picture of the Blessed Virgin on one side and write:

> Mary, Mother of my God,
> Be my Mother fair;
> Guard my little soul from sin,
> Keep me in your care.

6. Make this lesson a study of intimate home life. Have the children bring pictures of children kneeling in prayer and let them tell all they can about them. It may be well also to mention that those children whose mothers are too busy to pray with them, should not neglect to do so by themselves or with the younger children of the house.

7. Dramatize some of these intimate little scenes, going through the process of saying night prayer, examining conscience, begging mother's pardon for some fault, saying "Good night" to parents and other members of the family. The scenes might be repeated from day to day with variations suggested by the children, so that all will know exactly what to do in case the parents have not taken the trouble to teach them.

8. Make a class booklet on the Commandments of the Church.

9. By reference to Holy Scripture as given below, the teacher will tell the story in which the following texts appeared so that the child will understand each one in its setting:

"If thou wilt enter life, keep the commandments" (Matt. xix. 17).

"If you love Me, keep My commandments" (John xiv. 15).

"If you keep My commandments, you shall abide in My love;

as I also have kept My Father's commandments, and do abide in His love" (John xv. 10).

"And they were both just before God, walking in all the commandments and justifications of the Lord without blame" (Luke i. 6).

The children will memorize the text.

Pupils' Readings:

Catholic Educational Series, p. 45, "The Magic Ring"; p. 219, "Lessons for Life."

Religion, Second Course, MacEachen, Chap. 22, "Sin."

Teachers' References:

Practical Aids, p. 76, "Conscience."

Teachers' Notes:

IV. DOCTRINAL SUMMARY

The Commandments of God

The fundamental facts regarding the commandments of God, for children of this grade, have been covered. The questions at the end of each lesson have given the child the opportunity to look for the answers which enforce by repetition the principal facts and doctrine regarding the commandments of God. The form of the answer is guided by the form of the question. The children have now learned the doctrine. By way of summary and review, and giving the student's knowledge definite verbal form, the teacher will have the child learn the formulation of the truths taught in this unit as given in the catechism adopted in the diocese. These truths are:

Baltimore Catechism, No. 2.
    Questions 311, 312, 313, 314.[1]
Gasparri's Catechism, for Little Children, I.
    Question 4.
Gasparri's Catechism for Children, II.
    Questions 11, 27, 29, 30, 31, 32, 34, 35, 36, 37, 38.

---

[1]These questions and answers are given in the text, *The Life of the Soul.*

UNIT III
THE REDEMPTION

Time: From the second week in December to the first week in January, and from the second week in January to the first week in March, inclusive.

I. The Idea of the Redemption
II. The Messiah
III. The Baptism of Christ and the Trinity
IV. The Crucifixion and Resurrection

Feasts to Remember

December 8, Immaculate Conception
December 25, Christmas
December 28, Holy Innocents
January 1, New Year's Day
           Holy Name of Jesus
January 6, Epiphany
January 10, Holy Family
January 21, St. Agnes
February 2, Purification
February 11, Our Lady of Lourdes

Spiritual Crib for Christmas

First Week. Build stable and manger by many acts of obedience at home and in school (have manger and stable before the class on sand table or special table).

Second Week. Bring hay and straw by performing many acts of mortification and self-denial.

Third Week. Make the bedding for Jesus by acts of charity toward others. Visits to Jesus in the Blessed Sacrament.

Fourth Week. Garments for the Infant Jesus: Think often of the Baby Jesus and pray to Him.

I. The Idea of the Redemption

Pictures:

Expulsion of Adam and Eve from the Garden — Doré
The Immaculate Conception — Murillo
The Nativity — Correggio
The Crucifixion — Hofmann
The Resurrection, Easter Morning — Hofmann
The Ascension — Hofmann

Review:

Recall to the minds of the children the fall of our first parents, their punishment, and God's Promise of a Redeemer. Review Lessons 7 to 11 in *The Life of the Soul.*

Presentation:

When Adam and Eve died, they could not go to heaven because heaven was closed by their disobedience. But God, like a good Father, still loved them, even though He punished them. When He sent them away from Paradise, He promised them a Redeemer. They had to work hard, and suffer much in punishment for their sin: But they always remembered God's promise. They told their children that some day the Son of God would come to redeem them. Although Adam and Eve had disobeyed God, He would not send them to hell, for they were very, very sorry for what they had done and suffered much for their sins. God, therefore, put them into a place called Limbo, where they had to wait until the Redeemer would come. Their children died, and their children's children. All those who were good went to Limbo. We can imagine how glad Adam and Eve were to meet them all again. But still they could not be truly happy, because they could not see God and all the beautiful angels in heaven.

The people who lived on earth always remembered God's promise. They knew the Redeemer would come some time. But it was many, many years now since Adam and Eve were sent out of Paradise. When would the Redeemer come, they wondered. Oh, how the good people prayed to God please to send the Promised One soon. At last, after four thousand years of hoping and waiting, the Redeemer was born. The souls in Limbo heard the news, too, and oh, how eagerly they must have waited for Him to take them to heaven.

Explain to the children the meaning of Advent.

With this lesson begins the preparation for Christmas. At least two weeks before Christmas should be devoted to the activities suggested, and the work should continue for two more weeks after the Christmas holidays. Aim to instill into the hearts of the children a deep love for the Christ Child, and recall to their minds from time to time the Idea of the Redemption.

Use Lesson 21 in *The Life of the Soul* to summarize the work of the two weeks. Have the pupils prepare the lesson unusually well and give it as an important number in the Christmas program which should be the culmination of all the religious activities.

Lessons 22 and 23 may be read now after Christmas.

II. The Messiah

Review:

Where did Adam and Eve go after their death? Why could they not go to heaven? Could their children go to heaven? How long did they stay in Limbo? When did the Redeemer come? Who was the Redeemer?

Presentation:

Let the children read and tell in the order of their occurrence the stories connected with the birth of Christ. Add new pictures as the stories progress. Several weeks should be spent in preparation for Christmas. Bring it before the minds of the children again and again that Christ came as the promised Redeemer. Care should be taken that the stories and activities assume in the end a well-formed unit.

The Text:

Read Lesson 21, *The Life of the Soul* (The Promise of God Fulfilled).

The text will be used in this lesson as:

1. Introduction to the lesson.
2. Development of the lesson.
3. Summary of the lesson.
4. Review of the lesson.

Content: The particular content of this lesson will be found by pupils finding out answers to the following questions, or answering in the blank spaces the correct words:

God promised for man a .... or ....

The Son of God is the .... or ....

.... is His name.

He was born of the Virgin ....

He was conceived of the ....

His foster father was ....

Jesus was born in ....

Herod wanted to kill ....

Joseph took Mary and .... to Egypt.

After Herod died, Joseph brought Mary and .... from ....

Jesus lived in ....

Tell about the Wise Men of the East.

Tell what the angels did in this story.

How was Jesus lost, as Mary and Joseph thought?

Tell what Jesus did in the temple.

The Text:

Read Lesson 22, *The Life of the Soul* (Mary, Mother of God).

The text will be used in this lesson as:

1. Introduction to the lesson.
2. Development of the lesson.
3. Summary of the lesson.
4. Review of the lesson.

Content: The particular content of this lesson will be found by pupils finding out answers to the following questions, or answering in the blank spaces the correct words:

Mary is the .... of ....

Jesus is the Son of ....

.... is the mother of God.

Mary did not .... in her life.

Mary is .... of heaven.

Mary can help us with God.

Say five little prayers to Mary.

Make one prayer of your own.

Vocabulary: This vocabulary includes the words with religious content or associated with Scriptural narratives:

Lesson 21: Savior; announced; Jerusalem; Shepherds; Egypt; manger; Herod; doctors; temple; Nazareth; conceived; worship; Redeemer; Joseph; wisdom.

Lesson 22: Mary; pray; blessed; queen; Christians; prayers; Holy Ghost; angel; holy.

Suggestive Activities in Preparation for Christmas

1. Impress on the children's minds that Christ is the Messiah; that He is God and man; that He is the Son of God, the Second Person of the Blessed Trinity; that He always was God; that He became man for us.

Have the children learn some of the following or other appropriate hymns:

While Shepherds Watched
Holy Night
Dear Little One
Lovely Infant

2. Teach the ejaculation "Sweet Heart of Jesus, be my love."

3. Encourage the children to make visits to the Crib and remind them of the Christmas offering, their gift to the Redeemer.

4. Teach the Joyful Mysteries of the Rosary.

Encourage the children to do something to make poor children happy.

5. Let the class dramatize various Christmas scenes, such as The Annunciation, The Shepherds, The Magi, and use them for the Christmas Program.

6. For December 8, let the class draw a lily or make a lily poster.

7. Have the children make Christmas calendars, and Christmas cards with religious pictures, for their parents and friends.

8. Explain the meaning of the Christmas tree and ornaments.

9. Put up posters, drawings, language work, etc., in the classroom.

10. For the feast of the Presentation cut out or model a bird cage and birds. See *Art Education Through Religion,* Book II, p. 20.

11. The following are outstanding art pictures from which a number may be chosen for study or language work:

The Annunciation — Titian

Immaculate Conception — Murillo

The Nativity, Holy Night — Correggio

The Announcement — Plockhorst

Adoration of the Shepherds — Bougereau

The Worship of the Wisemen — Hofmann

Flight into Egypt — Plockhorst, Hofmann

The Presentation — Carpaccio

Repose in Egypt — Plockhorst

The Holy Family — Defregger

Childhood of Christ — Hofmann

Madonna and Child — Murillo

The Christ Child — Ittenbach

Christ in the Temple with the Doctors — Hofmann

Madonna and Child — Sickel

Sistine Madonna — Raphael

Bethlehem (*The Life of the Soul*, p. 48)

The Annunciation (*The Life of the Soul*, p. 50)

The Holy Family (*The Life of the Soul*, p. 52)

12. If possible set aside a corner of the classroom for a reading room. Have all the available religious books and pictures pertaining to the Christmas season on the table, where the children may have continual access to them. The religion and reading periods should at times be left for quiet reading and again for little group talks about the stories and pictures. Give the children the privilege of enjoying these books and pictures at any time during the day when their regular work is done.

13. Poems for study, reading, and language work:

"God, the Father" — Tabb

"Christmas Songs" — Lydia Ward

"The Holy Baby" — Father Faber

"Gates and Doors" — Joyce Kilmer

"The Christ Child" — Chesterton

"The Annunciation" — Adelaide Procter

"A Christmas Gift" — J. Quinn, S.J.

"The Lamb" — Wm. Blake

"Winter" — M. D. Thayer

"Catholic Nursery Rhymes" — Sister M. Gertrude

"The Name of Mary" — Adelaide Procter

"A Child's Prayer" — M. Betham Edwards

"Sleep Song" — D. McCarthy

"Christmas Time"

"Finding You" — M. D. Thayer

14. By reference to Holy Scripture as given below, the teacher will tell the story in which the following text appeared so that the child will understand it in its setting:

"This day is born to you a Savior who is Christ the Lord" (Luke ii. 11).

The children will memorize the text.

15. A great deal of the material for picture study, oral and written work, recitations, paper cutting, posters and creative work in clay, or drawing, may be drawn from these suggested readings:

Pupils' Readings:

American Reader, III, p. 166, "The Child's Thought at Christmas."

American Cardinal Reader, p. 15, "The Wonderful Message"; p. 19, "The Annunciation"; p. 51, "The Christ Child in the Temple"; p. 57, "The Frozen Hands"; p. 136, "St. Christopher."

Corona Reader, III, p. 134, "A Legend of the Christ Child"; p. 140, "The Nativity"; p. 237, "Holy Night."

De la Salle, III, p. 3, "The Holy Family"; p. 47, "Christ in the Temple"; p. 63, "Jesus in the Workshop"; p. 99, "The Child's Desire."

Daly, p. 125, "A Child's Christmas Story."

Ideal Catholic Reader, p. 15, "Christ Blessing the Little Ones"; p. 15, "A Birthday Gift," C. Rosetti; p. 125, "Little Jesus," Thompson.

Rosary Reader, III, p. 134, "When the King Came"; p. 219, "Shepherds of Bethlehem"; "Advent"; p. 172, "Palestine"; p.

176, "A House in Bethlehem"; p. 220, "Joel's Star."

Standard Catholic Reader, III, p. 79, "Star in the East"; p. 87, "Christmas Carol."

Cathedral, III, "Sweet Mother of Jesus."

Literature and Art, III, "Bethlehem"; "Christmas Night."

Teachers' References:

Practical Aids, p. 294, "Christmas Booklet"; pp. 99, 242, 243, "Drama, the Story of Christmas"; p. 91, "A Bed for the Infant"; p. 90, "Other Activities"; p. 190, "Christmas Program"; pp. 225, 287, "Poster"; p. 231, "Sandtable Project," "A Mission Project, Wise Men from the East"; p. 83, "The Life of Christ"; p. 98, "Longing for Jesus."

Art Education through Religion, II, p. 20.

The Holy Bible, St. Luke ii.

The Life of Christ, Spirago, pp. 179–183.

The Little Ones, p. 80, "Flight into Egypt"; p. 83, "Nazareth"; p. 87, "Lost in the Temple."

To the Heart of a Child, p. 37, "The Blessed Virgin"; p. 42, "The Annunciation"; p. 46, "Birth of the Messias"; p. 50, "The Magi"; p. 55, "The Holy Childhood."

Jesus of Nazareth, Mother Loyola, pp. 29–97, "The Promised One"; "The Hidden Life."

First Communion, Mother Loyola, p. 84, "Bethlehem"; p. 99, "Egypt"; p. 111, Nazareth."

Teachers' Notes:

III. The Baptism of Christ and the Trinity

For posters or mottoes the following may be used:

Glory be to the Father, and to the Son, and to the Holy Ghost.

Holy Ghost, come down upon Thy children.

See also Developments 1 and 2.

Pictures:
  Baptism of Christ — Perugino
  Behold the Lamb — Bida
  St. Joseph
  The Baptism of Christ (*The Life of the Soul,* p. 56)
Review:
Why did Jesus come to earth? How long did He stay with His parents at Nazareth? What did Jesus do in Nazareth? Most probably St. Joseph died before Jesus left His home to preach to the people. Then Jesus had to take His foster father's place in the workshop. Could St. Joseph go right to heaven when he died? Why not? Where did he go? Whom did he meet in Limbo? Do you think Adam and Eve and all the others were glad to meet St. Joseph? What do you suppose he told them?

Presentation:
Jesus stayed at home in Nazareth until He was thirty years old. Then He went out to preach to the people in order to show them the way to heaven, and to redeem them. That is why He came to earth. He wanted to open heaven for Adam and Eve and all of us, their children. He said good-by to His Mother, and went to the river Jordan where He met His cousin, John the Baptist.

Tell the story of the Baptism of Jesus. Point out the manifestation of the Blessed Trinity, the first appearance of the Holy Ghost.

Read Lesson 24 in *The Life of the Soul* until the children can repeat the sentences almost from memory.

Lesson 25 should follow the lesson on the Blessed Trinity, either this week, or next week, as time permits.

The Text:
Read Lesson 24, *The Life of the Soul* (The Blessed Trinity). The text will be used in this lesson as:
  1. Introduction to the lesson.
  2. Development of the lesson.
  3. Summary of the lesson.
  4. Review of the lesson.
Content: The particular content of this lesson will be found

by pupils finding out answers to the following questions, or answering in the blank spaces the correct words:

Jesus was .... years old when he was baptized.

John baptized ....

At the baptism of Christ the .... appeared as a dove.

At the baptism of Christ the .... spoke from a cloud.

The Blessed Trinity is one ....

The Blessed Trinity is one God in .... Divine Persons.

The Three Divine Persons are:

God the ....

God the ....

God the ....

God, the Father, is the .... Person of the Blessed Trinity.

God, the Son, is the .... Person of the Blessed Trinity.

How are we reminded of the Blessed Trinity when we bless ourselves?

The Text:

Read Lesson 25, *The Life of the Soul* (The Miracles of Christ)

The text will be used in this lesson as:

1. Introduction to the lesson.
2. Development of the lesson.
3. Summary of the lesson.
4. Review of the lesson.

Content: The particular content of this lesson will be found by pupils finding out answers to the following questions or answering in the blank spaces the correct words:

Christ lived how many years on earth?

Christ lived how many years after His baptism?

How old was Christ when He was baptized?

Christ, by the power of God, performed ....

He walked the ....

He .... the sick by His word only.

He made the blind ....

He made the lame ....

He cured ....
He raised men from the ....
He Himself rose from the ....
Christ is the .... of God.
Christ sits at the right .... of God in Heaven.

The Text:

Read Lesson 26, *The Life of the Soul* (Christ Loved Men).
The text will be used in this lesson as:

1. Introduction to the lesson.
2. Development of the lesson.
3. Summary of the lesson.
4. Review of the lesson.

Content: The particular content of this lesson will be found by pupils finding out answers to the following questions or answering in the blank spaces the correct words:

What are some of the things Christ did on earth?
He loved all of .... creatures.
He loved .... and women.
He loved boys and ....
He wanted us to .... God better.
He wanted us to keep the .... of God.
Tell one story of Christ's love of children from the Bible.

Vocabulary: This vocabulary includes only the words with religious content or associated with Scriptural narratives:

Lesson 24: river Jordan; beloved; John the Baptist; Blessed Trinity; dove; divine.

Lesson 25: miracles; ascended; disciples; wine; bread; blood; body.

Lesson 26: teaching; Kingdom of Heaven; Apostles; Peter; forbid.

Development:

1. Have the children cut or draw a dove, symbol of the Holy Ghost. Also a shamrock, symbol of the Trinity. Teach them that the Father, Son, and Holy Ghost are three distinct persons.

2. Make a visit to church with the class and show them the various symbols of the Holy Ghost and the Blessed Trinity that

may be found in the windows or the paintings on the altar rail or the pulpit.

3. Take this occasion to speak of devotion to St. Joseph, if you have not yet done so. A hymn to St. Joseph, such as "Dear Guardian of Mary," may be taught.

4. Tell the stories of St. Patrick and St. Augustine, referring to the Trinity. They might be dramatized.

5. Review the doctrine of the Blessed Trinity. Then let the children say the "Glory be to the Father, and to the Son, and to the Holy Ghost" while they reverently bow their heads.

6. Speak of the sign of the cross, reviewing it with the children and making any necessary explanation or correction. Encourage its reverent use, at prayer, when taking holy water, and in time of temptation.

7. The following poems may be read or taught:
"Holy Ghost Come Down Upon Thy Children" — Faber
"The Blessed Trinity" — Tabb

8. Other poems that may be taught:
"The Blessed Trinity" — Faber
"Every Child's Garden"; "St. Joseph"; "In the Workshop of St. Joseph"
"The Rann of the Three," from the Irish

9. Study the pictures in *The Life of the Soul*.
Raising the Daughter of Jaïrus (p. 60).
Christ and the Children (p. 62).

Pupils' Readings:
Corona Reader, III, p. 79, "Baptism of Jesus."
Religion, Second Course, MacEachen, p. 217, "The Baptism of Jesus."
Standard Catholic Reader, III, p. 186, "St. Patrick."

Teachers' References:
Jesus of Nazareth, p. 117, "The Banks of the Jordan."
Bible and Church History, Brother Eugene, p. 126, "Jesus Begins His Public Life."
Our Little Ones, p. 119, "The Trinity."
The Question Box, Father Conway, p. 238, "The Baptism of St. John the Baptist."

To the Heart of a Child, p. 59, "Beginning of the Public Life."
Teacher Tells a Story, Vol. I, p. 92, "The Trinity"; Vol. II,
p. 165, "At the Baptism of Jesus."
Teachers' Notes:

IV. The Crucifixion and Resurrection

Mottoes and Posters: Let the children choose their own
mottoes, preferably such as refer to the thought of the Redemption, as that is the underlying idea of the lesson.

Jesus died for me

Jesus died on the cross to redeem me

About three weeks should be devoted to the history of the
Passion and Resurrection. Lenten practices, Holy Week, and
Easter should all be considered during this time.

As an introduction to this lesson, read Lesson 20 in *The Life
of the Soul.*

Have the children memorize one or more of the following
poems:

"The Way of the Cross" — L. Feeney, S.J.

"The King's Highway" — Rev. Blunt

"O Sacred Cross" — William Cardinal O'Connell

Pictures:

The Crucifixion — Hofmann

Any other pictures of the Passion and Resurrection that are
available, particularly the pictures in *The Life of the Soul:*

The Last Supper (p. 64).

Christ Carrying the Cross (p. 68).

The Crucifixion (p. 70).

The Resurrection (p. 72).

The Ascension (p. 74).

Review:

How did Jesus begin His public life? Who was John the Baptist? What did the voice from heaven say? How long did Jesus remain on earth? Why did He come to earth?

Presentation:

After preaching to the people for three years, healing the sick, and doing good wherever He went, it was time for Jesus to begin the great work of the Redemption. Jesus came down to earth to open heaven for us by His sufferings and death. Jesus is our leader. Let us follow Him now through His terrible sufferings, so that we may learn how much He had to suffer to redeem us. (See Development 2.)

Let the children read or tell, without too much detail, the successive stories of the Passion up to the death and burial of Christ. It would be well to use the Stations of the Cross as a guide. (See Development 3.)

Now the time had come at last for which Adam and Eve and all their children had waited and prayed for so long. While the body of Jesus rested in the grave, His soul went to Limbo to visit all the souls that were waiting for Him to open heaven. Just think what joy there must have been in Limbo when Jesus showed Himself to all the holy souls, beginning with Adam and Eve, who had been there for thousands of years. Now they knew that God's promise which He made in Paradise was fulfilled: "I will put enmities between thee and the woman, and thy seed and her seed. She shall crush thy head, and thou shalt lie in wait for her heel." (See Development 4.)

For other Lenten activities see Developments 5 to 10.

Read Lesson 28, *The Life of the Soul,* and Lesson 30 as a review during the remaining time before Easter.

The Text:

Read Lesson 27, *The Life of the Soul* (The Holy Eucharist). The text will be used in this lesson as:

1. Introduction to the lesson.
2. Development of the lesson.
3. Summary of the lesson.
4. Review of the lesson.

Content: The particular content of this lesson will be found by pupils finding out answers to the following questions or answering in the blank spaces the correct words:

Christ wished to keep the Jewish . . . . of the . . . .

Christ established a new . . . . on this very night.

Christ established the . . . .

Who was present?

What is the day called?

What did Christ do with the bread?

What did He say?

What happened?

Christ gave power to priests to change in the . . . . the bread and wine into His Body and Blood.

When does this happen?

The Holy Communion we receive is not bread but the . . . . and . . . . of Jesus Christ.

Holy Communion is a source of . . . .

Grace comes from . . . .

Christ instituted the . . . .

We receive the Body and Blood of Christ in the Sacrament of . . . .

The Body and Blood of Christ is the . . . . of the soul.

Make a brief prayer such as is given in the last sentence of this story.

The Text:

Read Lesson 28, *The Life of the Soul* (Christ Suffers for Sins of Men).

The text will be used in this lesson as:

1. Introduction to the lesson.
2. Development of the lesson.
3. Summary of the lesson.
4. Review of the lesson.

Content: The particular content of this lesson will be found by pupils finding the answers to the following questions, or answering in the blank spaces the correct words:

What happened on Holy Thursday?

What happened on Good Friday?

What happened on Easter Sunday?

What happened after Easter Sunday?

Who said, "I find nothing to punish Him for"?

To whom was it said?

Of whom was it said?

Who said, "Crucify Him, crucify Him"?

To whom was it said?

Of whom was it said?

Who said, "Father forgive them for they know not what they do"?

To whom was it said?

Of whom was it said?

Christ died for our . . . .

Christ died for . . . . sins.

Look in the prayer book for the Stations of the Cross, and see how many of these events are pictured there.

Vocabulary: This vocabulary includes only the words with religious content or associated with Scriptural narratives:

Lesson 27: Holy Eucharist; Egypt; plotting; Jewish; impossible; Holy Communion; spiritual; Jews; Promised Land; Judas; New Law; chalice; mystery; lamb; priests; betray; broke; Mass; host.

Lesson 28: governor; crucified; thorns; vinegar; Mount Calvary; resurrection; Pontius Pilate; crucify; cross; forgive; sepulcher; judge; scourged; crowned; nailed; Good Friday; Easter Sunday.

Development:

1. Let the children make Lenten Posters, Three Crosses on Calvary, Agnus Dei, *Religion Through Art,* Book II, pp. 25, 31; see also the sand-table project in *Practical Aids,* p. 232.

Let them draw or cut symbols of the Passion: spear, crown, nails, cross, etc. Look for these in church and write a sentence about the meaning of the symbols.

2. Encourage the children to perform little acts of self-denial during Lent for love of the suffering Jesus. Remind them often of these little acts, which they might suggest, and have them

check up occasionally to see whether they have performed them faithfully.

3. Teach the children how to say the Stations with devotion. The little booklet, *Stations of the Cross for Children,* by Religious of the Cenacle, may be utilized here.

4. Have the children use the following texts as they relate the story:

"Thomas answered and said to Him: My Lord, and my God" (John xx. 28). Refer to the very appropriate use of these words after Holy Communion.

"I am the living Bread which cometh down from heaven" (John xiv. 2).

"And if I shall go, and prepare a place for you, I will come again, and will take you to Myself: that where I am, you also may be" (John xiv. 3).

"This day thou shalt be with Me in Paradise" (Luke xxiii. 43).

5. Let the children tell what Jesus probably said to the souls in Limbo and what they said to Him.

6. Have the class write or say the words of the Apostles' Creed that refer to the Redemption.

7. You might let the pupils make a Lenten Resolution Book: "My Lenten Gifts to Jesus."

8. Teach them the following prayers and hymns: "My Jesus, mercy! Save me by Your Precious Blood." "Eternal rest give unto them, O Lord, and let perpetual light shine upon them." "Hail Holy Queen," the sorrowful mysteries of the Rosary which are said during Lent, and also the glorious mysteries of the Rosary which are to be said after Easter.

9. Talk to the children about the obligation of Catholics to make their Easter Duty.

10. By reference to Holy Scripture as given below, the teacher will tell the story in which the following text appeared so that the child will understand it in its setting:

"Jesus answered, and said to him: If anyone love Me, he will keep My word, and My Father will love him, and We will come to him, and will make Our abode with him" (John xiv. 23).

The children will memorize the text.

11. Other poems that may be used for study or reading:

"O Sacred Cross" — William Cardinal O'Connell

"Thy Will be Done" — *Every Child's Garden*

"Crowned with Thorns" — *ibid.*

"Christ is Risen" — *ibid.*

Pupils' Readings:

American, III, p. 1, "The Gift of the Master."

Corona, III, "Our Lord and our Lady."

Ideal Catholic Reader, p. 23, "The Last Supper."

Rosary, III, p. 16, "The Cross"; p. 36, "The Sign of the Cross"; p. 86, "Crosses"; p. 133, "Jewish Money"; p. 174, "Jewish Feasts"; I, II, p. 207, "The Sabbath Feast"; p. 238, "The Passover"; p. 256, "The Crucifix."

Standard Catholic, III, p. 207, "An Easter Legend."

Wonder Stories of God's People, p. 268, "Hosanna to the Son"; p. 276, "The Last Supper"; p. 287, "Judas the Traitor"; p. 291, "In the Garden of Olives"; p. 298, "On the Hill of Calvary"; p. 305, "Christ is Risen."

Teachers' References:

The Holy Bible, John xiv, xx; Luke xxiii.

Art Education Through Religion, II, p. 25, 31.

Practical Aids, p. 232; p. 113, "The Sufferings and Death of our Lord."

The Little Ones, p. 134, "Entry into Jerusalem"; p. 110, "Calvary"; p. 113, "Easter Day."

To the Heart of a Child, p. 98, "The Last Supper"; p. 104, "The Passion"; p. 107, "The Resurrection."

Jesus of Nazareth, Mother Loyola, p. 307, "Jerusalem"; Mother Loyola, p. 322, "The Night in which He was Betrayed"; p. 343, "It is Finished."

First Communion, Mother Loyola, p. 229, "The Last Supper"; Mother Loyola, p. 245, "Calvary."

Sunday School Teacher's Explanation of the Catechism, Rev. Urban, Lesson 8, "Our Lord's Passion, Death, Resurrection."

Teacher Tells a Story, Vol. I, *"The Resurrection";* Vol. II, p. 142, "Burial, Descent into Limbo"; Vol. II, p. 110, "Obedience to Authority"; Vol. II, p. 148, "The Resurrection, Ascension, Last Judgment."

Teachers' Notes:

V. DOCTRINAL SUMMARY

Christ, The Redeemer

The fundamental facts regarding Christ, the Redeemer, for children of this grade, have been covered. The questions at the end of each lesson have given the child the opportunity to look for the answers which enforce by repetition the principal facts and doctrine regarding Christ, the Redeemer. The form of the answer is guided by the form of the question. The children have now learned the doctrine. By way of summary and review, and giving the student's knowledge definite verbal form, the teacher will have the child learn the formulation of the truths taught in this unit as given in the catechism adopted in the diocese. These truths are:

Baltimore Catechism, No. 2.

Questions 21, 23, 24, 25, 26, 27, 28, 30, 50, 60, 61, 62, 70, 75, 76, 77, 78, 79, 80, 81, 82, 83.[1]

Gasparri's Catechism, for Little Children, I.

Questions 8, 9, 10, 11, 13, 22.

---

[1]These questions and answers are given in the text, *The Life of the Soul.*

UNIT IV
THE CHURCH

Time: From the second week in March to the first week in April, inclusive.

I. Peter and the Power of the Keys.
II. The Catholic Church.
III. The Holy Eucharist.
IV. What the Priest does at Mass.
V. How can I be Saved.

Feasts to Remember

March 19, St. Joseph
Seven Sorrows
Palm Sunday
Holy Thursday
Good Friday
Easter Sunday

I. Peter and the Power of the Keys

For posters or mottoes:
"Feed My lambs, feed My sheep."
"Thou art Peter and upon this rock I will build My Church."
See also Development 1.

Pictures:
Christ and the Fisherman — Zimmermann
Pope Pius XI (*The Life of the Soul*, p. 82)

Review:
Why did Jesus suffer and die for us? On what day did He die for us? Where did His soul go while His body was in the grave? On what day did He rise from the dead?

Presentation:
After Jesus rose from the dead, His work on earth was nearly

78

done. He had shown the people how to live; He had taught them many beautiful lessons; finally, He had suffered and died to redeem them. Now He was getting ready to go back to heaven to His Father, where He promised to make a beautiful home for us all. Jesus did not wish to stay on earth forever, therefore He gave St. Peter and the other Apostles charge of teaching the people the way to heaven. He gave them wonderful powers. Today we shall see some of the powers He gave to them, especially to St. Peter. (See Development 2.)

Tell the story of St. Peter's being chosen as an Apostle, and Christ's words to Him: "Thou art Peter, and upon this rock I will build My Church." Explain the words as simply as possible. Relate also Christ's commission to St. Peter after the Resurrection. Deal particularly on the Primacy of Peter and the power Christ gave him. "Feed My lambs, feed My sheep." By that Jesus meant that Peter should take charge of those who believed what Jesus taught to the Apostles. (See Development 3.)

Read and discuss in connection with the following lesson on the Church, *The Life of the Soul*, Lessons 30 and 31.

Let the children make a "Vocation Booklet." The quotation: "Go ye and teach all nations" might serve as a keynote: Christ's Kingdom on earth, the work of the missionaries, pictures of children from all nations may be depicted in it. Let the pupils make their own suggestions. (See also Developments 8 and 9.)

II. The Catholic Church

Pictures:

Christ's Charge to St. Peter — Raphael

Descent of the Holy Spirit — Fra Angelico

The First Pentecost (*The Life of the Soul*, p. 80)

Review:

What did Jesus say to show that He wanted St. Peter to be the head of the Church? What promises did Jesus make to him? Did He mean He was going to put up a building of stone? What wonderful powers did Jesus give to His Apostles?

Presentation:

While Jesus was still on earth teaching the people and healing the sick, He was also training His Apostles to continue His work. Jesus did not wish to remain on earth always. Therefore He told the Apostles what to do when He should be gone. He taught them many things and gave them great powers. He told them that they must go out and teach the people the way to heaven as He had done. When Jesus had told them all He wanted them to do, He ascended into heaven. The Apostles were all afraid of the Jews. They hid themselves. But Jesus had promised that He would send them the Holy Ghost to help and enlighten them. Ten days after Jesus had gone to heaven, the Holy Ghost came down upon the Apostles in the form of fiery tongues. Then they became strong and brave. They no longer hid themselves but went out and preached to the people. That was on Pentecost Day, the birthday of the Church. St. Peter told the people that He whom they had crucified, was the Son of God. Three thousand were converted by his first sermon. They were the first Christians, that is, people who believe in Christ. They formed the first members of the Church. (See Development 4.)

The Apostles went from place to place and taught the people all that Jesus had told them. The other Apostles always went to St. Peter to ask questions and tell about their work, because He was the head of the Church. By and by St. Peter and the other Apostles ordained priests and bishops, so that when they themselves should die, others would be there to take their places. In this way, the Church kept on spreading over the whole earth. We Catholics belong to that Church, the true Church founded by Jesus Himself. We should be very happy to belong to the true Church. Many people have never heard of the Catholic Church. We should also pray for those who do not belong to it. (See Developments 5, 6, and 7.)

Read Lesson 29, *The Life of the Soul,* and point out that in the complete Creed is contained all that the Catholic Church believes and teaches. We say the Creed to show that we want to be true children of the Church and believe all that she teaches.

Things to find out: When did you become a member of the Catholic Church? What do we call the person who takes the place of St. Peter as head of the Church on earth? Where does the Pope live? How many Apostles were there present on Pentecost Day?

For other suggestions see Developments 10, 11, and 12.

Development:

1. Quotations to use:

"Thou art Peter and upon this rock I will build My Church" (Matt. xvi. 18).

"Lord, Thou knowest that I love Thee" (John xxi. 15).

"Feed My lambs; feed My sheep" (John xxi. 15–17).

"Fear not: from henceforth thou shalt catch men" (Luke v. 10).

"In My Father's house there are many mansions" (John xiv. 3).

2. Cut out or draw the keys of St. Peter. Write under them, Feed My lambs; feed My sheep.

Speak of the calling to the priesthood or sisterhood to go out and teach for Jesus.

3. Let the children find pictures and symbols in church, pertaining to St. Peter's keys and the foundation of the church.

4. Have some of the children relate to the class the stories of the Ascension and Pentecost.

5. Say a prayer with the class to thank God that we are children of the true Church and ask Him to keep us true to the Church until we die.

6. Let the class make a sand-table project of the Church in Africa, China, Alaska, etc.

7. Remind the children always to be reverent in church, to raise the hat when passing the church, to renew the baptismal vows, to be loyal to the church, to pray for the pope, heathens, missionaries.

8. Form a missionary club to make offerings for mite boxes, to choose friends among Catholics only, and to try to bring non-Catholics to church.

9. Give the class a chance to develop originality and initiative by letting them make a large chart, illustrated with pictures, showing the following comparisons: Sea — the world; net — the Church; fishermen — the pope, bishops, and priests.

10. For language work let the class write names of objects they see in a Catholic Church.

11. The following poem may be taught:

"Spring" — M. D. Thayer

12. Let pupils tell from mission magazines of the great sacrifices missionaries make to help spread the Church.

13. By reference to Holy Scripture as given below, the teacher will tell the story in which the following texts appeared so that the child will understand each one in its setting:

"And I say to thee: That thou art Peter; and upon this rock I will build My church, and the gates of hell shall not prevail against it.

And I will give to thee the keys of the kingdom of heaven. And whatsoever thou shalt bind upon earth, it shall be bound also in heaven: and whatsoever thou shalt loose on earth, it shall be loosed also in heaven" (Matt. xvi. 18, 19).

"Going therefore, teach ye all nations; baptizing them in the name of the Father, and of the Son, and of the Holy Ghost.

"Teaching them to observe all things whatsoever I have commanded you: and behold I am with you all days, even to the consummation of the world" (Matt. xxviii. 19, 20).

The children will memorize the text.

Pupils' Readings:

De la Salle, III, p. 102, "The Children and the Pope."

Rosary, III, p. 28, "Peter's Pence"; p. 39, "The Bishop of Rome"; p. 38, "St. Peter"; p. 53, "Genuflection"; p. 40, "The Vatican"; p. 147, "The Cathedral of Cologne."

Standard Catholic Reader, III, p. 124, "In a Catholic Church"; p. 100, "Sister Marguerite."

Ideal Catholic Reader, p. 94, "The Children's Friend."

Corona, III, p. 31, "Calling of the Disciples."

Religion, Second Course, pp. 70–72, MacEachen, "Christ Founded the Catholic Church," "And the Catholic Church."

Teachers' References:

To the Heart of a Child, p. 158, "The Church"; p. 167, "The Marks of the Church"; p. 174, see diagram.

Tells Us Another, Father Herbst, p. 44, "We Don't Talk in Church"; p. 133, "He is always There"; "Of Course, God is always Present."

Teacher Tells a Story, Vol. II, pp. 168–175; "The Holy Catholic Church"; pp. 176–180, "Communion of Saints."

Jesus of Nazareth, M. Loyola, "The Catholic Church."

The Catechism Explained, Spirago, p. 251, "Communion of Saints"; p. 264, "Purgatory"; pp. 221–246.

The Holy Bible, Matt. xvi. 18; John xxi. 15; John xxi. 15–17; John xiv. 3; Luke v. 10.

Teachers' Notes:

III. The Holy Eucharist

Poster or blackboard mottoes:

Blessed be God

My God and My All

Holy, Holy, Holy

This lesson is a short preparation for a study of the Mass which follows:

These two lessons should lead directly to the more immediate preparation for First Holy Communion and should be intimately associated in the children's minds with our Lord's coming into their hearts. Teach them to make a short spiritual communion each day at Mass.

Pictures:

The Last Supper — Da Vinci

Miracle of the Loaves and Fishes — Hofmann

The Last Supper (*The Life of the Soul,* p. 64)

Review:

Whom did Jesus make the Head of the Church on earth? What did Jesus say to Peter? What did Jesus promise to do for His Church? Where is Jesus now? How can we tell that Jesus is present on the altar?

Presentation:

Once when Jesus was on earth, He told the people He would give them Bread from Heaven. Someone will tell us the story.

Tell or have the children tell the story of the Multiplication of the Loaves, also the story of the Last Supper, pointing out that Christ instituted the Holy Eucharist on that occasion. Dwell particularly on our Lord's love for us. He wished to stay with us always. He knew we would need Him. He wished to come to us in Holy Communion. (See Development 1.)

Dwell on the promise of our Lord, "The bread that I will give is My flesh, for the life of the world." When Jesus and His disciples were at the Last Supper this wonderful promise was to come true. Jesus knew that He would be leaving this world soon. He knew that the Jews would put Him to a terrible death. But He loved men so much that instead of being angry with them and planning a terrible punishment He planned to stay with them always. At the Last Supper Jesus changed the bread and wine into His own Body and Blood. He knew we would need Him and so He left us His Body and Blood as our food on the journey of life. This Body and Blood of Jesus is called the Holy Eucharist. Jesus is always present on the altar under the form of the host. We cannot see Him face to face but He is there, and He waits for us day after day in the little tabernacle, and He seems to say to us as He did to those whom He fed in the desert: "He that eateth my Flesh and drinketh My blood abideth in Me and I in Him" (John vi. 57). Shall we let Him wait without ever going to visit Him or receiving Him into our hearts? Jesus is already waiting for you. Will you not tell Him, too, that you long for Him? Let us say the little prayer together:

> Jesus, Jesus, come to me,
> Oh, how much I long for Thee.

See Development 2.

Read Lesson 27, *The Life of the Soul,* carefully and review it several times in the course of the next two weeks. Have the pupils memorize the more important sentences, especially the last which should be used often as a prayer.

IV. What the Priest Does at Mass

Keep before the children by means of posters or blackboard mottoes such thoughts as the following:

My Lord and my God

This is My Body, this is My Blood

Pictures:

The Last Supper — Da Vinci

The Priest at Consecration (*The Life of the Soul,* p. 106)

Any picture of the Mass, especially the Elevation.

Review:

How did Jesus feed the thousands of people in the desert? What did He say to them? When did He change the bread and wine into His Body and Blood? Why did Jesus change bread and wine into His Body and Blood?

Presentation:

When Jesus changed bread and wine into His own Body and Blood at the Last Supper, He was saying the very first Mass that was ever said. When He had finished, He told His Apostles to do as He had done. He said, "Do this in commemoration of Me." Ever since that time the Apostles and their successors, the bishops and priests, have been changing the bread and wine on the altar during Mass into the Body and Blood of Jesus. Just think what a wonderful miracle happens every day when you are at Mass. The priest takes the place of Jesus: and at the Consecration he holds the white host in his hands and says: "This is My Body." Then he takes the chalice with wine and says: "This is My Blood," and at the same moment the bread and wine are changed into the Body and Blood of Jesus. (See Development 3.)

Explain in a simple way the Sacrifice of the Mass, gradually getting the children to follow the more important parts. By all means get into their hands the kind of Mass Book that insures interest, understanding, and devotion. (See also Developments 4 to 8.)

Development:

1. Find symbols of the Blessed Sacrament in Church and in religious books. Draw, cut out, or mold some of these symbols.

2. Let the children memorize some of the following quotations:

"This is the Bread which cometh down from heaven, that if any man eat of it, he may not die" (John vi. 50).

"Thomas answered and said to Him: My Lord and My God" (John xx. 28).

"In like manner the chalice also, after He had supped, saying: This is the chalice, the new testament in My blood, which shall be shed for you" (Luke xxi. 19, 20).

"If any man eat of the Bread, he shall live for ever; and the Bread that I will give, is My Flesh, for the life of the world" (John vi. 52).

"My little children, let us love not in word, nor in tongue, but in deed and in truth" (John iii. 18).

3. Teach the children to look up at the Host and chalice at Elevation and to say as St. Thomas did: "My Lord and my God."

4. Have the class make a Mass Booklet: See *Practical Aids,* p. 295, and *Art Education Through Religion,* Book II, pp. 35–39.

5. Recall the obligation of all Catholics to attend Mass every Sunday and holyday of obligation.

6. Poems for study:

"Finding You" — M. D. Thayer

"Thoughts" — M. D. Thayer

7. Teach the following prayers and their use during Mass:

May the Almighty and Merciful God grant us pardon, absolution, and remission of our sins.

Let us give thanks to the Lord our God.

Lamb of God who taketh away the sins of the world have mercy on us.

8. Explain the term "sacrifice," and show how the Sacrifice of the Altar is the same as the Sacrifice of the Cross.

Pupils' Readings:

Religion, Second Course, Chapter 34, "The Sacrifice of the Mass"; Chapter 35, "Also the Real Presence."

My Mass Book, Sister Servants of the Immaculate Heart of Mary.

The Life on Earth of Our Blessed Lord, "In the Tabernacle."

Teachers' References:

The Holy Bible, John, chapters iii, vi, xx; Luke, chapter xxii.

The Mass, Rev. Joseph Denney.

Art Education Through Religion, II, pp. 35–39.

Practical Aids, p. 295.

Teachers' Notes:

V. How Can I Be Saved

Suggestions for mottoes and posters:

Grace is the life of the soul

Hail, full of grace

Pictures:

Expulsion of Adam and Eve — Doré

The Annunciation — Titian

Nativity — Correggio

The Crucifixion — Hofmann

Christ's Charge to Peter — Raphael

Review:

How did God make Adam and Eve? Were Adam and Eve happy when God first made them? Why were they sent out of

Paradise? What sin did all people inherit from Adam and Eve? Who alone was preserved from original sin?

Presentation:

After God had made Adam out of the slime of the earth, He breathed a soul into him. That soul had a wonderful gift which gave it life. It was the gift of grace. Grace is the life of the soul. Nothing can take the beautiful gift of grace from the soul except mortal sin. When Adam and Eve sinned they lost the gift of grace which God had given them. That is why they could not go to heaven. Mortal sin is often called the death of the soul because it takes away the life of divine grace.

If we wish to go to heaven, we must have grace for our souls. When children are born they have not the gift of grace because they have original sin on their souls. The Blessed Virgin Mary alone was preserved from original sin. Her soul was filled with grace. That is why the angel said to her: "Hail, full of grace." (See Development 1.)

But since all people are born without grace, how can they be saved and go to heaven? Who gives us grace? When Jesus died on the cross for us, He brought grace down from heaven. He left this grace with the Church and the Church gives it to us by means of the sacraments. There are seven sacraments. They are: Baptism, Confirmation, Holy Eucharist, Penance, Extreme Unction, Holy Orders, and Matrimony. We shall see what these sacraments do for the soul. (See Development 2.)

In Baptism we receive divine grace for the first time. When we are baptized, we are said to be born again because we receive the life of grace for our soul. Confirmation makes the life of grace strong in our soul. The Holy Eucharist nourishes the life of grace in our soul. The Sacrament of Penance heals the soul again when we have committed sin. Extreme Unction strengthens grace in us so that we may die a happy death. The Sacrament of Holy Orders gives us priests to care for the life of grace in our souls. The Sacrament of Matrimony gives us a Christian home so that we may live a life of grace.

Read about the sacraments in your religion book, *The Life of the Soul,* Lesson 31. (See also Developments 3 and 4.)

The Text:

Read Lesson 32, *The Life of the Soul* (Why Christ Came to Earth.)

The text will here be used as a summary of the lesson.

Content: The particular content of this lesson will be found by pupils finding out answers to the following questions or answering in the blank spaces the correct words:

List five things Christ came to do.

What is a sacrament?

What do the sacraments give to the soul?

How many sacraments are there?

What sacrament makes us Christians?

What sacrament forgives our sins?

What sacrament gives us nourishment?

What sacrament makes us soldiers?

What sacrament gives grace to the dying?

What sacrament gives grace to people when they are married?

What sacrament gives grace to men when they are ordained priests?

.... instituted the Sacrament of Baptism.

.... instituted the Sacrament of Penance.

.... instituted the Sacrament of Holy Eucharist.

.... instituted the Sacrament of Confirmation.

.... instituted the Sacrament of Extreme Unction.

.... instituted the Sacrament of Matrimony.

.... instituted the Sacrament of Holy Orders.

Christ instituted the .... sacraments.

Vocabulary: This vocabulary includes the words with religious content or associated with Scriptural narratives.

Roman Catholic Church; Baptism; Penance; Extreme Unction; ordained; sacraments; instituted; Confirmation; Matrimony; Holy Orders.

Development:

1. Have the children tell the story of the Annunciation.

2. Learn the seven sacraments and tell which of them you have received.

3. Have the children read or memorize the following poems:

"The Child's Prayer" — M. Betham Edwards

"Because He Loves Us" — A. Cary

"It is Finished" — Christina Rosetti

4. Fill in the words: life; heaven; sin; grace; Mary.

    (1) Grace is called .... of the soul.

    (2) Mortal sin takes away .... from the soul.

    (3) .... was full of grace.

    (4) We are all born without grace because we have ......
        on our souls.

    (5) We cannot go to .... without grace.

5. By reference to Holy Scripture as given below, the teacher will tell the story in which the following text appeared so that the child will understand it in its setting:

"I am the Door. By Me if any man enter in, he shall be saved: and he shall go in and out, and shall find pastures — I am the Good Shepherd. The Good Shepherd giveth His life for His sheep — I am the Good Shepherd; and I know Mine, and Mine know Me" (John x. 9, 11, 14).

"I am the Way, and the Truth, and the Life. No man cometh to the Father but by Me" (John xiv. 6).

The children will memorize the text.

Pupils' Readings:

Spiritual Way, Book I, pp. 31–41, "God's Light"; Book II, pp. 82–105, "The Failure."

Religion, Second Course, II, MacEachen, p. 74, "Divine Grace."

Teachers' References:

To the Heart of a Child, p. 179, "Sanctifying Grace."

Sunday School Teacher's Explanation of the Catechism, Rev. A. Urban, pp. 170–185, "Grace."

Teachers' Notes:

VI. DOCTRINAL SUMMARY

The Church of Christ

The fundamental facts regarding the Church of Christ, for children of this grade, have been covered. The questions at the end of each lesson have given the child the opportunity to look for the answers which enforce by repetition the principal facts and doctrine regarding the Church of Christ. The form of the answer is guided by the form of the question. The children have now learned the doctrine. By way of summary and review, and giving the student's knowledge definite verbal form, the teacher will have the child learn the formulation of the truths taught in this unit as given in the catechism adopted in the diocese. These truths are:

Baltimore Catechism, No. 2.
    Questions 114, 116, 117, 118, 120.[1]
Gasparri's Catechism, for Little Children, I.
    Questions 12, 14.
Gasparri's Catechism for Children, II.
Questions 44, 45, 46.

---

[1]These questions and answers are given in the text, *The Life of the Soul.*

UNIT V
THE SACRAMENTS

Time: From the second week in April to the first week in June, inclusive.

I. Baptism.

III. Confession.

V. Holy Communion.

VII. Confirmation.

Feasts to Remember

Ascension Thursday

Pentecost Sunday

Corpus Christi

Sacred Heart

I. Baptism

The following may be used as a blackboard motto or poster: Baptism maks me a child of God.

Have the children make a "Sacrament Booklet" and write in it how to baptize. Keep the booklet for three other sacraments.

Pictures:

Baptism of a Child (The Life of the Soul, p. 88).

Review:

With what sin does the soul come into the world? Why is every child born with original sin on his soul? Can anyone go to heaven with original sin on his soul? What great gift of God must the soul have to go to heaven? Who earned the great gift of grace for us? To whom did Jesus leave His grace? How does the Church give grace to the people?

Presentation:

Every child is born with original sin. It is not a child of God. The sacrament that takes away original sin and gives grace to the soul is Baptism. Parents take their children to church to be baptized as soon as possible so that they may not die with original sin on their soul. Baptism makes us children of God by giving us grace. After Baptism the soul is holy and pure. Nothing can harm it, except sin. Mortal sin, you know, takes away grace from the soul. (See Development 1.)

Baptism can be received only once. Jesus gave the Apostles the power to baptize. He said: "Going, therefore, teach ye all nations: baptizing them in the name of the Father, and of the Son, and of the Holy Ghost." The priest gives us the Sacrament of Baptism, but when there is danger that a person may die without Baptism anyone may baptize. Perhaps some day you may have a chance to save a soul by baptizing it, if a priest cannot be called. That is why we shall all learn how to baptize. When the priest baptizes he uses baptismal water to baptize. That is water which was blessed on Easter Saturday or on the Saturday before Pentecost. When we baptize we should use clear water, pour it on the head of the person we are baptizing and at the same time while we are pouring say: "I baptize thee in the name of the Father, and of the Son, and of the Holy Ghost." (See Development 2.)

When you were baptized your godparents promised in your name that you would keep from evil all your life. Later on you will make that promise in your own name, because you could not do so yourself when you were a tiny baby. Sometimes people are not baptized until they are grown up. Then Baptism takes away from their soul not only original sin, but also all other sins. In that case they must be sorry for their sins, just as when they go to Confession. They must also promise never to commit sin again. (See Development 3.)

Explain Baptismal Vows: In Baptism God promised you: I take you as My child. — If you remain a child of God, I will take you to heaven. Your godparents answered for you because you were too small: I will always remain a child of God. This solemn promise is called the Baptismal Vow. (See Developments 4 and 5.)

Developments 6 to 8 will give further suggestions for activities
Read *The Life of the Soul*, Lessons 32 and 33.

The Text:

Read Lesson 33, *The Life of the Soul* (Baptism, Grace in the Soul).

The text will be used in this lesson as:

1. Introduction to the lesson.
2. Development of the lesson.
3. Summary of the lesson.
4. Review of the lesson.

Content: The particular content of this lesson will be found by pupils finding out answers to the following questions or answering in the blank spaces the correct words:

What sin was on the baby's soul when it came into this world?

This is the effect of whose disobedience?

Who showed the way to restore God's grace to the soul?

What is this way called?

Which is the first Sacrament we receive?

Baptism prepares for the other ....

Baptism gives .... to the soul.

Baptism makes us .... of God.

Baptism wipes out .... sin.

In Baptism .... is poured on the head of the person baptized.

While this is being done the priest says: I .... thee in the name of the Father, and of the Son, and of the Holy Ghost.

What is the outward sign in Baptism?

The Text:

Read Lesson 34, *The Life of the Soul* (The Mark of the Christian).

The text will be used in this lesson as:

1. Introduction to the lesson.
2. Development of the lesson.
3. Summary of the lesson.
4. Review of the lesson.

Content: The particular content of this lesson will be found by pupils answering in the blank spaces the correct words:

Baptism gives .... to the soul.

Baptism leaves a .... in the soul.

It is the mark of a ....

This mark can never be ....

Baptism makes us ....

Baptism wipes away all .... from the soul.

Baptism is the gateway to all the ....

Baptism starts us on the Highway to ....

Vocabulary: This vocabulary includes the words with religious content or associated with Scriptural narrative:

Lesson 32: baptizing; sign.

Lesson 33: gateway; mark.

Development:

1. Tell the story of Queen Blanche and King Louis of France. Let the children dramatize the scene.

2. Let the children learn how to baptize by using a doll to represent the baby, *not* a pencil, ruler or other object. Be sure that a spirit of reverence prevails.

3. Let the children find and tell stories of saints who kept their baptismal innocence.

4. Make an act of thanksgiving with the children for having been made a child of God at Baptism.

5. Have the pupils tell the story of the Baptism of Jesus.

6. *Things to find out:* Who are your godparents? What did they do for you at Baptism? What name did you get in Baptism? In what church were you baptized?

7. Suggest to the children to renew their baptismal vows every year on their birthday. "Dear Jesus, I promise You, as my god-parents did for me on the day of my Baptism, that I will always remain a child of God. Mother Mary, help me keep my promise. Dear Guardian Angel watch over me and help me."

8. Poems to learn:

"Baptism" — *Every Child's Garden*

"God's Priests" — *ibid.*

"Thy Kingdom Come" —*ibid.*

9. Inquire at home and learn some facts about your own baptism.

Make a chart covering these facts:

The date of my Baptism was ....
The name of the church in which I was baptized is ......
....
The names of my godparents are ....
My baptismal patron saints are ....
Their feasts are ....
Something I like about my patron saint's life is..........
....

10. By reference to Holy Scripture as given below, the teacher will tell the story in which the following text appeared so that the child will understand it in its setting:

"Going therefore teach ye all nations: baptizing them in the name of the Father, and of the Son, and of the Holy Ghost" (Matt. xxviii. 19).

"Jesus answered: Amen, amen I say to thee, unless a man be born again of water and the Holy Ghost, he cannot enter into the Kingdom of God" (John iii. 5).

The children will memorize the text.

Pupils' Readings:

The Wonder Gifts — Taggart

The Sacraments — Father Kelly, Baptism

Teachers' References:

Teacher Tells a Story, Vol. II, Story Number, pp. 58, 66, 67, 101, 119, 120, 125, 128, 130, 135, "Baptism."

Sunday School Teacher's Explanation of the Catechism, Rev. Urban, p. 202, "Baptism."

To the Heart of a Child, p. 65, "Baptism."

Practical Aids, p. 148, "Gratitude of Little Apostles"; p. 146–154, "The Child Apostolate."

The Holy Bible, Matthew, chapter xxviii.

Teachers' Notes:

II. DOCTRINAL SUMMARY

The Sacrament of Baptism

The fundamental facts regarding the Sacrament of Baptism, for children of this grade, have been covered. The questions at the end of each lesson have given the child the opportunity to look for the answers which enforce by repetition the principal facts and doctrine regarding the Sacrament of Baptism. The form of the answer is guided by the form of the question. The children have now learned the doctrine. By way of summary and review, and giving the student's knowledge definite verbal form, the teacher will have the child learn the formulation of the truths taught in this unit as given in the catechism adopted in the diocese. These truths are:

Baltimore Catechism, No. 2.
Questions 136, 137, 138, 152, 156.[1]
Gasparri's Catechism, for Little Children, I.
Questions 15, 16.
Gasparri's Catechism for Children, II.
Questions 127, 133, 135, 136.

III. Confession

If the children have already gone to confession, take this occasion to review the sacrament thoroughly.

At least two weeks should be devoted to the lesson on confession which will naturally include a review of the commandments and examination of conscience.

For study, review, and further development, make the fullest possible use of Lessons 30 to 38 in *The Life of the Soul.* Let the children refer to their books continually and use the lessons as a guide for the examination of conscience and confession of sins.

Pictures:
Prodigal Son — Molitor
Prodigal Son (The Life of the Soul, p. 94)

---

[1]These questions and answers are given in the text, *The Life of the Soul.*

Peter and the Apostles (*The Life of the Soul,* p. 96)
Priest in the Confessional (*The Life of the Soul,* pp. 102 and 103)

Review:

How is original sin taken from the soul of man? How often can we receive Baptism? What great gift does the person baptized receive in Baptism? Who obtained the gift of grace for us from heaven? Do people always keep grace in their souls after Baptism? How do they lose grace?

Presentation:

Many people fall into sin again after Baptism. They lose the grace of God and cannot go to heaven. What are they going to do? God knew that we would not all be strong enough to keep His grace always in our souls. But He does not want us to lose our souls. He loves us too much. He made us for heaven and He wants to give us every chance to get there. Therefore He gave us another sacrament to take away sin from our soul. It is the Sacrament of Penance. (See Development 1.)

How good God is to give us so many helps to get to heaven. Just think how many signs He has put on the road of life to show us the way. He gave us Baptism to take away original sin. He gave us the commandments to point the way to Him, and now we have another sacrament to help us in case we fall into sin. (See Development 2.)

The Text:

Read Lesson 36, *The Life of the Soul* (The Soul at Seven Years).

The text will be used in this lesson as:
1. Introduction to the lesson.
2. Development of the lesson.
3. Summary of the lesson.
4. Review of the lesson.

Content: The particular content of this lesson will be found by pupils answering in the blank spaces the correct words:

The soul at the time we are born does not have ....

In Baptism the soul received ....

In Baptism the soul receives the .... of the Christian.

The soul does not lose the grace of Baptism until it disobeys God's commandments .... in an .... matter.

Grace can be .... to the soul in a way Christ showed the Apostles.

Grace can be restored to the soul by having our .... forgiven.

The priests of the Catholic Church in the name of Christ, were given the power to .... sin by Christ Himself.

The Text:

Read Lesson 37, *The Life of the Soul* (The Power to Forgive Sins).

The text will be used in this lesson as:

1. Introduction to the lesson.
2. Development of the lesson.
3. Summary of the lesson.
4. Review of the lesson.

Content: The particular content of this lesson will be found by pupils answering in the blank spaces the correct words:

There are two kinds of sins; .... and ....

If we disobey God in .... matter when we .... what we are doing, but do it ...., we ....

This is a .... sin.

If we disobey God when one of these three things is not true of our act, the sin is a .... sin.

To be a .... sin, we must know what we are doing.

To be a .... sin, we must disobey God's law in an .... matter.

To be a .... sin, we must disobey .... one of God's commandments.

When did Christ give the Apostles the power to .... sins?

In the Sacrament of .... our sins are forgiven.

Our sins are forgiven by the words of .... of the priest.

The words of absolution of the priest are the outward .... of the Sacrament of Penance.

The Text:

Read Lesson 38, *The Life of the Soul* (The Keys of the Kingdom of Heaven).

The text will be used in this lesson as:
1. Introduction to the lesson.
2. Development of the lesson.
3. Summary of the lesson.
4. Review of the lesson.

Content: The particular content of this lesson will be found by pupils finding out answers to the following questions:

Who said the following:
1. "As the Father hath sent Me, I. also send you."
2. "Receive ye the Holy Ghost."
3. "Thou art Christ, the Son of the Living God."
4. "And I will give to thee the keys of the Kingdom of Heaven, and whatsoever thou shalt bind upon earth, it shall be bound also in heaven, and whatsoever thou shalt loose on earth, it shall be loosed in heaven."

To whom were the above words said?

Who was the first Pope?

Who made Peter the head of the Church?

The Text:

Read Lesson 39, *The Life of the Soul* (Confession of Sins).

The text will be used in this lesson as:
1. Introduction to the lesson.
2. Development of the lesson.
3. Summary of the lesson.
4. Review of the lesson.

Content: The particular content of this lesson will be found by pupils finding out answers to the following questions or by answering in the blank spaces the correct words:

The sinner who truly . . . . for his sins may have them forgiven.

The way to forgiveness is always . . . .

This simple and easy way is to go to . . . .

What are the five things necessary for a worthy confession?

Vocabulary: This vocabulary includes only the words with a religious content or associated with Scriptural narratives:

Lesson 36: promised; innocent; naughty; deliberately.

Lesson 37: venial; mortal; peace; absolution.

Lesson 38: prophet; pope; rock; keys; bind; loose.

Lesson 39: confessional; examination of conscience; committed; contrition; penance; sorrow.

Development:

1. Dramatize the Prodigal Son and other stories. Let the children try to find the essentials of confession in this story.

2. Have the children tell the story of the Institution of the Sacrament of Penance.

3. Have the children learn one or more of the following quotations:

"If you will not forgive men, neither will your Father forgive you" (Matt. vi. 15).

"If you will enter into life, keep the Commandments" (Matt. xix. 17).

"Jesus answered and said to him: If anyone love Me, he will keep My word, and My Father will love him, and We will come to him, and will make Our abode with him" (John xiv. 23).

4. Have the children talk about some of the following or similar pictures that are available:

Christ and the Sinner — Hofmann

The Good Shepherd — Plockhorst

The Divine Shepherd — Murillo

Mary Magdalen — Hofmann

Christ the Consoler — Plockhorst

Crucifixion — Guido Reni

Denial of St. Peter — Harrach

St. Peter Repentant — Dolci

The Good Thief — Hofmann

5. Talk on frequent confession and on proper behavior while going to confession; for example, waiting their turns, not going at a time when older people need the time, praying while waiting.

6. Continue the "Sacrament Booklet." Write in it the five steps necessary for confession.

7. Poems to read or study:

"Going to Confession," p. 52, *Every Child's Garden.*

"God's Home," E. F. Garesché, S.J. (*The Life of the Soul,* p. 97).

8. By reference to Holy Scripture as given below, the teacher will tell the story in which the following text appeared so that the child will understand it in its setting:

"If thou wilt enter into life, keep the Commandments" (Matt. xix. 17).

"If you will not forgive men, neither will your Father forgive you your offenses" (Matt. vi. 15).

"Master, which is the great commandment in the law? Jesus said to him: Thou shalt love the Lord thy God with thy whole heart, and with thy whole soul, and with thy whole mind. This is the greatest and the first commandment. And the second is like to this: Thou shalt love thy neighbor, as thyself. On these two commandments dependeth the whole law and the prophets" (Matt. xxii. 36–40).

The children will memorize the text.

Pupils' Readings:

A Child's Garden of Religion Stories, pp. 123–127, "The Ten Commandments"; p. 155, "A Brass Serpent"; p. 232, "Against the Devil and Sin."

American Catholic Reader, III, p. 161, "The Little Gray Lamb."

Columbia Reader, III, p. 76, "The Sacrament of Penance"; p. 36, "What are Your Faults"; p. 69, "The Prodigal Son"; p. 155, "The Good Samaritan."

Ideal Catholic Reader, III, p. 151, "Why Rose Couldn't Sleep"; p. 104, "Jesus Heals the Lepers"; p. 228, "The Prodigal Son."

Rosary Reader, III, p. 234, "The Good Shepherd"; p. 246, "The Prodigal Son."

Our Sacraments, Father Kelly, pp. 26–45, "Penance."

Teachers' References:

The Holy Bible, Matthew, chapters vi, xix; John, chapter xiv.

Our Little Ones, p. 122, "Confession"; p. 106, "Martha and Mary"; p. 110, "Calvary."

Practical Aids, pp. 77, 92, 123.

First Communion, Chapter 25, "The Wedding Garment"; Chapter 26, "The Lost Sheep."

First Confession, Mother Loyola.
The Children's Charter, pp. 3–44, Mother Loyola.
Teacher Tells a Story, Vol. 1, pp. 123–147; p. 107; pp. 94–101; Vol. II, p. 181.
The Faith for Children, M. Eton, p. 129.
To the Heart of a Child, p. 86.
The Catechism Explained, Spirago, pp. 605, 639, "Penance."
A Sunday School Teacher's Explanation of the Catechism, Rev. Urban, pp. 230–257, "Penance."

Teachers' Notes:

IV. DOCTRINAL SUMMARY

The Sacrament of Penance

The fundamental facts regarding the Sacrament of Penance, for children of this grade, have been covered. The questions at the end of each lesson have given the child the opportunity to look for the answers which enforce by repetition the principal facts and doctrine regarding the Sacrament of Penance. The form of the answer is guided by the form of the question. The children have now learned the doctrine. By way of summary and review, and giving the student's knowledge definite verbal form, the teacher will have the child learn the formulation of the truths taught in this unit as given in the catechism adopted in the diocese. These truths are:

Baltimore Catechism, No. 2.
   Questions 136, 137, 138, 187, 191.[1]
Gasparri's Catechism, for Little Children, I.
   Questions 18, 19, 20.
Gasparri's Catechism for Children, II.
   Questions 127, 161, 162, 166.

---

[1] These questions and answers are given in the text, *The Life of the Soul.*

V. Holy Communion

With this lesson begins the immediate preparation for First Holy Communion, or more intensive study of this sacrament in case the children have already received Holy Communion.

Again, *The Life of the Soul* should serve as a guide for the preparation for Holy Communion. Lessons 39 to 43 should be read and discussed and read again. They contain practically all the material necessary for a thorough understanding and a worthy reception of the Holy Eucharist.

Pictures:

Miracle of Loaves and Fishes — Murillo

Child Receiving First Communion, (*The Life of the Soul,* p. 110)

Review:

What does Baptism do for the soul? Confession? Tell some of the many things God has done for us to help us on the road to heaven? Where is Jesus now? When does He come down on the altar? Why is He in the tabernacle? Review Lesson 27, *The Life of the Soul.*

Presentation:

Jesus comes down on the altar in every Holy Mass when the priest changes bread and wine into His Body and Blood. He stays with us on the altar, but even that is not enough. He wants to come still closer. He wants to come to each one of us in Holy Communion. He wants to come into our hearts. Our soul must be pure and holy when our Lord comes to us in Holy Communion. Those who have a mortal sin on their souls must go to confession before they receive Jesus. We prepare to receive Jesus in Holy Communion by prayer. We also fast from midnight before we go to Holy Communion. To fast means to take no food or drink. By not taking food or drink, we show our respect for the Blessed Sacrament. Jesus waits for us in the Tabernacle. He loves to come into the hearts of good children. Do we ask Him to come often? Do we show our love for Him by telling Him how much we want to receive Him? Are we trying every day to make our hearts better and more holy? We shall learn these days how to get ready for the coming of Jesus. After Holy Communion we thank Jesus for having come to us. He is in our heart. We pray to Him and He blesses us.

We may go to Holy Communion every day. The Church.commands that we go to Holy Communion once a year at Easter time. It would be a mortal sin not to go to Holy Communion during Easter time each year.

The Text:

Read Lesson 41, *The Life of the Soul* (The Holy Eucharist). The text will be used in this lesson as:

1. Introduction to the lesson.
2. Development of the lesson.
3. Summary of the lesson.
4. Review of the lesson.

Content: The particular content of this lesson will be found by pupils finding out answers to the following questions, or answering in the blank spaces the correct words:

Grace is the .... of the soul.

What is the food of the soul?

What power have priests of the Roman Catholic Church?

When do they exercise this power?

What is the outward sign of the Sacrament of the Holy Eucharist?

The Text:

Read Lesson 42, *The Life of the Soul* (Holy Communion). The text will be used in this lesson as:

1. Introduction to the lesson.
2. Development of the lesson.
3. Summary of the lesson.
4. Review of the lesson.

Content: The particular content of this lesson will be found by pupils finding out answers to the following questions, or answering in the blank spaces the correct words:

In Holy Communion we receive the .... and .... of Christ.

In the Mass, the bread and wine are changed into the .... and .... of Christ.

We must be in the state of grace to receive ....
....

We must have .... from midnight to receive Holy Communion.

What two conditions are necessary to receive Holy Communion?

Which of the following practices will you try to follow:

1. We may go to Holy Communion once a day.
2. We should go to Communion weekly, or at least monthly.
3. We must go to Communion once a year, at Easter time, to be a practical Catholic.

The Text:

Read Lesson 43, *The Life of the Soul* (Christ Speaks to the Soul).

The text will be used in this lesson as:

1. Introduction to the lesson.
2. Development of the lesson.
3. Summary of the lesson.
4. Review of the lesson.

Content: The particular content of this lesson will be found by pupils finding out answers to the following questions:

Write a number of sentences that you think Christ might say to your soul.

The Text:

Read Lesson 44, *The Life of the Soul* (The Soul Speaks to Christ).

The text will be used in this lesson as:

1. Introduction to the lesson.
2. Development of the lesson.
3. Summary of the lesson.
4. Review of the lesson.

Content: The particular content of this lesson will be found by pupils finding answers to the following:

Write a number of sentences which tell how your soul feels toward Christ, particularly after Holy Communion.

The Text:

Read Lesson 46, *The Life of the Soul* (Before Confirmation).

The text will be used in this lesson as:

1. Introduction to the lesson.
2. Development of the lesson.
3. Summary of the lesson.
4. Review of the lesson.

Content: The particular content of this lesson will be found by pupils finding out answers to the following question:

When do we begin life as Christians?

What sacrament starts us on King's Highway as a Child of God?

What precious gift is given to us in Baptism?

What do we call the guideposts and rules along the King's Highway?

When we keep the commandments what do we show to God?

When we disobey the commandments what happens to our soul?

After we have lost grace by mortal sin how do we find it again?

What sacrament restores grace to our soul after we have lost it by disobeying the commandments?

What is the sacrament that is food for our souls?

How does the Holy Eucharist make our souls in the sight of God?

How are we helped if we receive the Holy Eucharist often?

Vocabulary: This vocabulary includes the words with religious content or associated with Scriptural narratives.

Lesson 41: life; species.

Lesson 42: altar; thanksgiving; sacrifice.

Lesson 43: flesh; multiply; God; shepherd; refresh.

Lesson 44: name.

Development:

1. Teach the hymn "O Lord, I am Not Worthy," or another appropriate hymn for Holy Communion; also "A Child's May Hymn."

Let the children sing other hymns in honor of the Holy Ghost or the Guardian Angel to ask their help. Especially beautiful and appropriate are: *Hymns for First Communion,* Sisters of St. Francis, Dubuque, Iowa.

2. Teach some of the following prayers:
Jesus Teach Me How to Pray.
Acts before and after Holy Communion.
My Lord and my God.
May the Body and Blood of our Lord Jesus Christ pre-
serve my soul to everlasting life.
Jesus in the most Holy Sacrament, have mercy on us.

3. Have quotations on the blackboard every day and let the
children use them often.

"This is the Bread which cometh down from heaven: that if
any man eat of it, he may not die" (John vi. 50).

"I am the living Bread which cometh down from heaven"
(John vi. 51).

"But Jesus said to them: Suffer the little children, and forbid them not to come to Me: For the Kingdom of Heaven is for
such" (Matt. xix. 13, 14).

"If any man eat of this Bread, he shall live for ever: and the
Bread that I will give, is My flesh for the life of the world"
(John vi. 52).

"And Jesus said to them: I am the Bread of Life: He that
cometh to Me shall not hunger and he that believeth in Me shall
never thirst" (John vi. 35).

"As the Father hath loved Me, I also have loved you. Abide
in My love" (John xv. 9).

4. Remind the children often to think of Jesus in the Blessed
Sacrament, to visit Him and to ask Him to come into their
hearts.

5. Encourage the class to pray for the parents of their Communion classmates, especially for the conversion of those not
practicing their religion.

6. Have them make a special gift to Jesus each day in the
form of a sacrifice, visit, or prayer.

7. Make much of having the parents to go to Holy Communion with their children on First Communion Day.

8. Have children make a booklet throughout the time of
preparation:

My First Communion

Jesus, My Best Friend

My Prayer Book

9. Suggest to the children that they make a Spiritual Garden in the form of a booklet:

Roses: Attention and Order

Lilies: Prayers and Holy Masses

Violets: Silence

Forget-me-nots: Ejaculations to Jesus

Carnations: Obedience

Let each child choose one special flower to represent the correction of a secret fault.

10. Encourage children to save money for the mite box from their own little earnings and let them perform some work of charity with the savings.

11. Let the pupils collect and mount pictures of Holy Communion and post them on the bulletin board.

12. Have the class compose little prayers for before and after Holy Communion and write them into their booklets.

13. Cut a Basket of Fish: See *Religion Through Art*, I, p. 31.

14. Poems for study or reading:

"A Child's Wish" — Rev. A. J. Ryan (*The Life of the Soul*, p. 108)

"Because He Loves Us" — Alice Cary

"First Communion" — M. D. Thayer

"After Communion Day" — Faber

"At My Heart's Door" — *Every Child's Garden*, p. 4

"Holy Mass" — *ibid.*, p. 37

"First Holy Communion" — *ibid.*, p. 40

"My Lord and My God" — *ibid.*, p. 43

"Talk to Jesus" — *ibid.*, p. 45

"Thy Little One" — Christina G. Rosetti (*The Life of the Soul*, p. 115)

"Heaven" — Father Faber (*The Life of the Soul*, p. 116)

"After Communion" — Mary Dixon Thayer (*The Life of the Soul*, p. 112)

15. By reference to Holy Scripture as given below, the teacher will tell the story in which the following text appeared so that the child will understand it in its setting:

"Thomas answered, and said to Him: My Lord, and my God" (John xx. 28).

"If any man eat of this Bread, he shall live forever; and the Bread that I will give, is My flesh, for the life of the world" (John vi. 52).

"Lord, I am not worthy that Thou shouldst enter under my roof: but only say the word, and my soul shall be healed" (Matt. viii. 8). (From the Mass. This passage is based on Matt. viii. 8, where the Centurion says to Christ: "Lord I am not worthy that Thou shouldst enter under my roof: but only say the word, and my *servant* shall be healed.")

The children will memorize the text.

Pupils' Readings:

A Child's Garden of Religion Stories, Chapters 28 to 30, 31, 33.

American Catholic Reader, III, p. 84, "My New Sister."

A Child's Catholic Reader, III, p. 248, "St. Clare"; p. 250, "Jesus Rewards His Beloved"; p. 271, "Imelda."

Corona, III, p. 177, "Jesus, Gentlest Savior"; p. 91, "Jesus and the Little Child"; p. 87, "To the King of Heaven."

Columbia Reader, III, p. 112, "Holy Communion"; p. 118, "The Lily"; p. 250, "Today."

Ideal Catholic, III, p. 72, "Miracle of the Loaves"; p. 11, "God Heard Fred's Prayers"; p. 38, "First Communion"; p. 149, "The Sacred Heart."

Bible Stories for Little Children, p. 119, S. A. Louis; p. 121, "The Promise."

Our Sacramentals, Father Kelly, p. 46, "Bread from Heaven."

Our First Communion, Father Kelly.

Standard Catholic Reader, Thaxter, III, "Spring"; p. 130, "A Legend of a Fair Child."

Teachers' References:

The Holy Bible, John, chapters vi, xv; Matthew, chapter xix.

First Communion, Mother Loyola, Parts II and III.

Children's Charter, Mother Loyola, Part II.

The Life of Our Lord, Mother Salome, pp. 289–365.

Eucharistia, J. Kramp, S.J. (N.B. Eucharistic Education, 1.190); also the Sacrificial Banquet, 69.

Practical Aids, pp. 126–133, "Blessed Sacrament Section, VI."

The Little Ones, p. 76, "The Blessed Sacrament"; p. 131, "Feeding the Five Thousand"; pp. 135, 138, 139–142, "The Last Supper."

To the Heart of a Child, p. 93, "The Loaves and Fishes"; p. 98, "The Last Supper."

Jesus of Nazareth, Mother Loyola, pp. 329–334, "The Last Supper."

Teacher Tells a Story, Vol. I, 109–122, "Communion."

Encyclical on Holy Communion.

Practical Aids, p. 246, "Legend of the Christ Child"; p. 128, "Sacred Heart."

Tell Us Another, Rev. Herbst, "Stories for First Communion," pp. 58, 84, 88, 95, 98, 107, 124, 127, 134.

See list of Catholic books, *Catholic School Journal*, November, 1931.

Tell the children or have them read about saints noted for their love of the Blessed Sacrament; e.g., Tarcisius, Imelda, Little Nellie of Holy God, St. Aloysius, St. Gerard.

Teachers' Notes:

VI. DOCTRINAL SUMMARY

The Sacrament of the Holy Eucharist

The fundamental facts regarding the Sacrament of the Holy Eucharist, for children of this grade, have been covered. The questions at the end of each lesson have given the child the opportunity to look for the answers which enforce by repetition the principal facts and doctrine regarding the Sacrament of Holy Eucharist. The form of the answer is guided by the form of the question. The children have now learned the doctrine. By way of summary and review, and giving the student's knowledge definite verbal form, the teacher will have the child learn the formulation of the truths taught in this unit as given in the catechism adopted in the diocese. These truths are:

Baltimore Catechism, No. 2.
Questions 136, 137, 138, 238, 239, 240, 252, 253, 254, 260, 262, 263, 265.[1]
Gasparri's Catechism, for Little Children, I.
Questions 21, 22, 23, 24, 25, 26.
Gasparri's Catechism for Children, II.
Questions 127, 140, 141, 148, 151.

VII. Confirmation

Pictures:
Descent of the Holy Ghost — Fra Angelico
Bishop putting Chrism on Forehead (*The Life of the Soul,* p. 122)
Bishop Slapping Cheek (*The Life of the Soul,* p. 124)
Review:
How many persons are there in God? When did God the Son appear on earth? When did the Holy Ghost appear for the first time? When did He come again? In what form? What did the Holy Ghost do for the Apostles? How did the Apostles act before the Holy Ghost came down upon them?
Presentation:
Read Lesson 31, *The Life of the Soul.* (See Development 1.) The same Holy Ghost who came down upon the Apostles on Pentecost will come to you also when you receive the Sacrament of Confirmation. You may not feel that He is there, but He will put into your heart the courage and strength to live up to your

---

[1]These questions and answers are given in the text, *The Life of the Soul.*

religion and to fight bravely against sin. In the Sacrament of
Baptism we received grace for the first time; in Penance we
can find grace again if we have lost it. In Confirmation we receive a special grace by which we become soldiers of Christ.
Confirmation is given by the bishop and leaves a mark on our
soul which will remain there forever. Those who receive Confirmation must be in the state of grace; that is, they may not
have a mortal sin on their souls.

Read *The Life of the Soul*, Lesson 47, for the necessary explanation and discuss the lesson with the class.

For further activities see Developments 2 to 5.

The Text:

Read Lesson 47, *The Life of the Soul*.

The text will be used in this lesson as:

1. Introduction to the lesson.
2. Development of the lesson.
3. Summary of the lesson.
4. Review of the lesson.

Content: The particular content of this lesson will be found
by pupils finding out answers to the following questions:

Find as many reasons as you can why Christ instituted the
Sacrament of Confirmation.

How are we prepared for Confirmation?

Who can confirm?

What does the bishop do in Confirmation?

What does the bishop say in confirming a person?

Why does the bishop give each person confirmed a gentle blow
on the cheek?

The Text:

Read Lesson 48, *The Life of the Soul* (The Holy Ghost).

The text will be used in this lesson as:

1. Introduction to the lesson.
2. Development of the lesson.
3. Summary of the lesson.
4. Review of the lesson.

Content: The particular content of this lesson will be found
by pupils answering in the blank spaces the correct words:

The Holy Ghost is the .... Person of the Blessed Trinity.

The Holy Ghost is ....

We receive in Confirmation the .... and .... of the Holy Ghost.

The graces and gifts of the Holy Ghost make us .... as soldiers.

The graces and gifts of the Holy Ghost prepare us for the .... of life.

The graces and gifts of the Holy Ghost make us ready to tell our .... in God.

The graces and gifts of the Holy Ghost make us ready to show our .... for God.

The Text:

Read Lesson 49, *The Life of the Soul* (The Mark of the Soldier of Christ).

The text will be used in this lesson as:

1. Introduction to the lesson.
2. Development of the lesson.
3. Summary of the lesson.
4. Review of the lesson.

Content: The particular content of this lesson will be found by pupils answering in the blank spaces the correct words:

Confirmation, like Baptism, leaves on the soul a ....

This mark cannot be ....

This mark lasts ....

Two of the sacraments that leave a mark on the soul are .... and ....

Confirmation, like Baptism, can be received but ....

Two Sacraments that can be received but once are .... and ....

Holy Communion can be received ....

Development:

1. Have pupils look up and tell the story of the first Pentecost.

2. Review the prayers to the Holy Ghost explaining their significance and teach a hymn or poem in honor of the Holy Ghost in preparation for Pentecost.

3. Find in readers the lives of great heroes and heroines of the Church who had the strength to die for their faith.

Vocabulary: This vocabulary includes the words with religious content or associated with Scriptural narratives:

Lesson 44: temptations; archbishop; confirmed; salvation; bishop; parish; chrism.

4. Dramatize a scene from the story of some martyr.

5. Speak of the feast of the Pentecost, the birthday of the Church, when it is celebrated.

6. Write the following facts if you have been confirmed:

 a) The date of your Confirmation.

 b) The name of the bishop who confirmed you.

 c) The name of the church in which you were confirmed.

 d) The name of your sponsor.

 e) The name you chose.

7. By reference to Holy Scripture as given below, the teacher will tell the story in which the following text appeared so that the child will understand it in its setting:

"Then they laid their hands upon them, and they received the Holy Ghost" (Acts viii. 17).

"I will ask the Father, and He shall give you another Paraclete, that He may abide with you for ever" (John xiv. 16).

The children will memorize the text.

Pupils' Readings:

American, III, p. 116, "The Little Lily of the Indians"; p. 16, "Bernadette"; "Finding a Way to Heaven."

Cathedral, III, "St. Agnes."

Columbus, III, p. 119, "St. Elizabeth of Hungary"; p. 219, "St. Philip Neri."

Corona, III, p. 11, "St. Joan of Arc"; p. 241, "St. Theresa."

De la Salle, II, p. 99, "The Holy Innocents."

Ideal, III, p. 116, "Our Heroes."

Literature and Art, III, "St. Sebastian the Soldier."

Standard Reader, II, p. 51, "St. Rose of Lima"; p. 60, "St. Cecelia."

Our Sacraments, Father Kelly, p. 64, "Christ's Soldiers."

Teachers' References:
The Catechism Explained, Spirago, pp. 584–589, "Confirmation."
Externals of the Catholic Church, pp. 52–58, Sullivan.
Teachers' Notes:

VIII. DOCTRINAL SUMMARY

·The Sacrament of Confirmation

The fundamental facts regarding the Sacrament of Confirmation, for children of this grade, have been covered. The questions at the end of each lesson have given the child the opportunity to look for the answers which enforce by repetition the principal facts and doctrine regarding the Sacrament of Confirmation. The form of the answer is guided by the form of the question. The children have now learned the doctrine. By way of summary and review, and giving the student's knowledge definite verbal form, the teacher will have the child learn the formulation of the truths taught in this unit as given in the catechism adopted in the diocese. These truths are:

Baltimore Catechism, No. 2.
   Questions 136, 137, 138, 166, 167, 168, 170, 172.[1]
Gasparri's Catechism, for Little Children, I.
   Question 17.
Gasparri's Catechism for Children, II.
   Questions 127, 137, 138.

---

[1]These questions and answers are given in the text, *The Life of the Soul.*

FINAL REVIEW

Spend the last weeks of school in completing and reviewing the lessons in *The Life of the Soul*.

Have the children select their favorite reading lessons, poems, and hymns for a special program to be given on the last day of school. As a final number let the class read slowly and reverently the Apostles' Creed, Lesson 51, and follow the program immediately by a little talk on their religious obligations during the summer. In order to make the occasion more impressive, small sheets of paper may be passed around with the following or similar sentences mimeographed on them or perhaps written by the children themselves:

I will obey my parents.

I will say my prayers every day.

I will go to Mass every Sunday.

I will go to Mass on the fifteenth of August, a holyday of obligation.

I will receive Jesus often in Holy Communion.

Ask each child to sign his name on the bottom of the paper and to pin the slip up at home where it will remind him daily of his obligations.

The Text:

Read Lesson 51, *The Life of the Soul* (I Go to Prepare a Place for You).

The text will be used in this lesson as:

1. Introduction to the lesson.
2. Development of the lesson.
3. Summary of the lesson.
4. Review of the lesson.

Content: The particular content of this lesson will be found by pupils finding out answers to the following questions or answering in the blank spaces the correct words:

List the proofs of Christ's love for us that you can give.

Now make a list of ways in which you can prove your love for Christ.

What do Christ's words mean: "Come to Me ....
.... you."

What place has Christ prepared for you?

What did Christ mean "In My Father's house"?

What do you think heaven is?

The Text:

Read Lesson 53, *The Life of the Soul* (The Apostles' Creed).

The text will be used in this lesson as:

1. Introduction to the lesson.
2. Development of the lesson.
3. Summary of the lesson.
4. Review of the lesson.

Content: The particular content of this lesson will be found by pupils answering in the blank spaces the correct words:

I believe in God the ....

I believe in God the ....

I believe in God the ....

I believe in the .... Church.

I believe in the .... of Saints.

I believe in the forgiveness of ....

I believe in the .... of the body.

I believe in .... everlasting.

Vocabulary: This vocabulary includes the words with religious content or associated with Scriptural narratives.

Communion of Saints

Development:

1. By reference to Holy Scripture as given below, the teacher will tell the story in which the following texts appeared so that the child will understand it in its setting:

"In My Father's house there are many mansions. If not, I would have told you: because I go to prepare a place for you" (John xiv. 2).

"This day thou shalt be with Me in Paradise" (Luke xxiii. 43).

"Not every one that saith to Me, Lord, Lord, shall enter

into the Kingdom of Heaven; but he that doth the will of My Father who is in Heaven, he shall enter into the Kingdom cf Heaven" (Matt. vii. 21).

The children will memorize the text.

RESOURCE LIST

We have collected on the following pages a comprehensive list of all the recommended resources found in this manual. Based on their content and/or their frequent use in this series (often across more than one grade level) we have indicated the most essential of these with an asterisk (*), while resources which may be found on the internet are marked with a cross (†).

Third Grade Teacher Resources

*† *The Holy Bible.*

† *The Baltimore Catechism #2* (unrevised/pre-1941)

The Catholic Catechism (Parts 1 and 2), Peter Cardinal Gasparri (London: Sheed & Ward, 1932).

* *Art Education through Religion,* Mary G. McMunigle (New York: Mentzer, Bush & Company, 1931).

A Book of Religion for Catholic Elementary Schools: Compendium of Bible and Church History, Brother Eugene, O.S.F., Litt.D. (New York: William H. Sadlier, 1927).

† *The Catechism Explained,* Rev. Francis Spirago (New York: Benziger Brothers, 1899).

† *The Catholic Education Series, Religion Book 3,* Thomas Edward Shields, M.A., Ph.D., LL.D. (Washington D.C.: The Catholic Education Press, 1915).

The Children's Charter, Mother Mary Loyola (New York: Burns And Oates, 1911).

Eucharistia, Rev. Joseph Kramp, S.J. (St. Paul: E.M. Lohmann Company, 1926).

Externals of the Catholic Church, Rt. Rev. John F. Sullivan (New York: P.J. Kenedy & Sons, 1917). (see note for *The Visible Church*)

The Faith for Children (from Seven to Fourteen), Mary Eaton (London: Sands & Co., 1925).

First Communion, Mother Mary Loyola (London: Burns & Oates, 1896).

First Confession, Mother Mary Loyola (New York: Benziger Brothers, 1902).

Jesus of Nazareth: The Story of His Life Written for Children, Mother Mary Loyola (New York: Benziger Brothers, 1906).

†*The Life of Our Lord Written for Little Ones*, Mother Mary Salome (London: Burns And Oates, 1900).

The Little Ones: A Course of Relgious Instruction for children up to eight years, Mary Eaton (London: Sands & Co., 1925).

The Mass, Joseph Aloysius Dunney (New York: The MacMillan Company, 1924).

Practical Aids for Catholic Teachers, Sr. Mary Aurelia, O.S.F., M.A. and Rev. Felix M. Kirsch, O.M.Cap., Litt.D. (New York: Benziger Brothers, 1928).

†*The Question-Box Answers*, Rev. Bertrand L. Conway (New York: The Catholic Book Exchange, 1903).

Religion First Course, Roderick MacEachen, D.D. (New York: The MacMillan Company, 1920).

The Spiritual Way, Books 1-3, Mother Margaret Bolton (Yonkers-on-Hudson: World Book Company, 1929-1930).

†*The Story Ever New*, Rev. James Higgins (New York: The MacMillan Company, 1920).

†*Sunday School Teacher's Explanation of the Baltimore Catechism*, Rev. A. Urban (New York: Joseph F. Wagner, 1908).

Teacher Tells a Story (2 volumes), Rev. Jerome D. Hannan, D.D. (New York: Benziger Brothers, 1925).

†*Teacher's Handbook to the Catechism (3 Volumes)*, Rev. A. Urban (New York: Joseph F. Wagner, 1902).

**Teaching the Ten Commandments*, S. Mary Agnesine, S. Mary Catherine, SSND (Milwaukee: Bruce Publishing Company, 1931).

*Tell us Another, Winfrid Herbst, S.D.S. (St. Nazianz: The Society of the Divine Savior, 1929).

* †*To the Heart of the Child*, Josephine Van Dyke Brownson (New York: The Universal Knowledge Foundation, 1918).

†*The Visible Church*, Rt. Rev. John F. Sullivan (New York: P.J. Kenedy & Sons, 1920). (*This is a rearrangement of the material found in the author's previous book, Externals of the Catholic Church.*)

Third Grade Student Readers

(This list is provided for reference purposes; the majority of recommended readings from these books has been included in a newly published anthology reader to accompany this series.)

The American Cardinal Reader, Book Three, Edith M. McLaughlin (New York: Benziger Brothers, 1929).

The American Second Reader for Catholic Schools, The School Sisters of Notre Dame (Boston: D.C. Heath and Company, 1928).

The American Third Reader for Catholic Schools, The School Sisters of Notre Dame (Boston: D.C. Heath and Company, 1928).

Cathedral Basic Readers, Book Three, Rev. John A. O'Brien, Ph.D. (Chicago: Scott, Foresman and Company, 1931).

The Catholic Education Series Third Reader, Thomas Edward Shields (Washington, D.C.: The Catholic Education Press, 1910).

Columbus Series Third Reading Book, W.T. Vylmen, Ph. D (New York: Schwartz, Kirwin & Fauss, 1899).

The Corona Readers, Book 3, James H. Fassett (Boston: Ginn and Company, 1912).

De la Salle Readers Second Grade, Brothers of the Christian Schools (New York: St. Joseph's Normal Institute, 1915).

De la Salle Reader Third Grade, Brothers of the Christian Schools (New York: St. Joseph's Normal Institute, 1916).

The Ideal Catholic Reader, Third Reader, A Sister of St. Joseph (New York: The MacMillan Company, 1916).

Literature and Art Books, Book Three, Bridget Ellen Burke (Boston: Educational Publishing Company, 1909).

The Rosary Readers Third Reader, Sister Mary Henry, O.S.D. (Boston: Ginn and Company, 1927).

Standard Catholic Readers, Second Reader, Mary E. Doyle (New York: American Book Company, 1909).

Standard Catholic Readers, Third Reader, Mary E. Doyle (New York: American Book Company, 1909).

Additional Student Reading for Third Grade

Bible Stories for Children, Sister Anna Louise, S.S.J. (New York: Schwartz, Kirwin & Fauss, 1919-1935).

**A Child's Garden of Religion Stories*, Rev. P. Henry Matimore, S.T.D. (New York: The Macmillan Company, 1929).

Every Child's Garden (Scranton: The New Hope, 1926).

**Heroes of God's Church*, Rev. P. Henry Matimore, S.T.D. (New York: The Macmillan Company, 1930).

**The Life on Earth of Our Blessed Lord*, Grace Keon (St. Louis: B. Herder, 1913).

My Mass Book, Sisters Servants of the IHM (New York: The MacMillan Company, 1929).

**Our First Communion*, Rev. William R. Kelly (New York: Benziger Brothers, 1925).

*Our Sacraments, Rev. William R. Kelly (New York: Benziger Brothers, 1927).

Religion Second Course, Roderick MacEachen, D.D. (New York: The MacMillan Company, 1922).

The Spiritual Way, Book 1, Mother Margaret Bolton (Yonkers-on-Hudson: World Book Company, 1929-1930).

Text-book of Religion, Book 3, Peter Christopher Yorke (San Francisco: The Text Book Publishing Company, 1901).

The Wonder Gifts, Marion Ames Taggart (New York: Benziger Brothers, 1923).

*Wonder Stories of God's People, Rev. P. Henry Matimore, S.T.D. (New York: The Macmillan Company, 1929).

THE HIGHWAY TO HEAVEN SERIES

Prepared in the Catechetical Institute of Marquette University

(In co-operation with a group of Priests and Sisters teaching in the elementary schools)

GRADE	TEXT	MANUAL CURRICULUM IN RELIGION *(1st to 8th Grade inclusive)*
I	**THE BOOK OF THE HOLY CHILD** By *Sister Mary Bartholomew, O.S.F.* 96 pages	First Grade Teachers Plan Book and Manual
2	**THE LIFE OF MY SAVIOR** By a School Sister of Notre Dame 196 pages	Second Grade Teachers Plan Book and Manual
3	**THE LIFE OF THE SOUL** Prepared in the Catechetical Institute of Marquette University *Edward A. Fitzpatrick, Ph.D.* Educational Director 144 pages	Third Grade Teachers Plan Book and Manual
4	**BEFORE CHRIST CAME** By a School Sister of Notre Dame 256 pages	Fourth Grade Teachers Plan Book and Manual
5	**THE VINE AND THE BRANCHES** By the *Rev. R. G. Bandas, Ph.D.Agg., S.T.D. et M.* and a School Sister of Notre Dame 320 pages	Fifth Grade Teachers Plan Book and Manual
6	**THE SMALL MISSAL**	Workbook for the Missal
7 & 8	**THE HIGHWAY TO GOD** Prepared in the Catechetical Institute of Marquette University *Edward A. Fitzpatrick, Ph.D.* Educational Director 420 pages	**Practical Problems in Religion** By the *Rev. R. G. Bandas, Ph.D.Agg., S.T.D. et M.* (Answers problems in text)